BACKTRACKING IN BROWN WATER

RETRACING LIFE ON MEKONG DELTA RIVER PATROLS

ROLLAND E. KIDDER

iUniverse LLC
Bloomington

BACKTRACKING IN BROWN WATER
RETRACING LIFE ON MEKONG DELTA RIVER PATROLS

iUniverse books may be ordered through booksellers or by contacting:

iUniverse LLC
1663 Liberty Drive
Bloomington, IN 47403
www.iuniverse.com
1-800-Authors (1-800-288-4677)

Because of the dynamic nature of the Internet, any web addresses or links contained in this book may have changed since publication and may no longer be valid. The views expressed in this work are solely those of the author and do not necessarily reflect the views of the publisher, and the publisher hereby disclaims any responsibility for them.

ISBN: 978-1-4917-2070-7 (sc)
ISBN: 978-1-4917-2072-1 (hc)
ISBN: 978-1-4917-2071-4 (e)

Library of Congress Control Number: 2014900595

Printed in the United States of America.

iUniverse rev. date: 01/28/2014

Table of Contents

Preface vii

Introduction.. ix

Road Trips ix

1. The Chief's Family...1

2. A Sister... 12

3. Training..22

4. Going and Coming... 31

5. On Patrol 38

6. The Vietnamese..53

7. Happenings...69

8. Warrior 80

9. Border Interdiction..98

10. Camping Out...115

11. Engineer... 131

12. Jimmy 152

13. R & R 168

14. Transition...180

15. Endgame.. 198

16. Vietnam Today 209

17. Flashback: The Chief..243

18. Requiem 251

Acknowledgements...265

Preface

This book is a reflection on another time spawned by my long-planned return trip to Vietnam in 2010. It combines the old with the new, the old being a year, 1969-1970 that I spent in the U.S. Navy in South Vietnam as a patrol officer in the Mekong Delta. This was intended only to be an article, "Backtracking in Brown Water", published in December 2010 by *Naval History* magazine. However, in researching for that article and in poring over a Journal that I had kept from those days, three names kept popping up: Eldon Tozer, Bob Olson and Jim Rost. They were all friends and fellow combatants in the war that was waged in the southern-most part of South Vietnam. They didn't make it home. Their names are engraved on the Vietnam Wall in Washington, D.C.

This is my story, not theirs. But my story would not be complete without also writing about them. They were all strong men and represented different aspects of the warfare that was going on. Eldon Tozer was, as I, a Navy PBR patrol officer. Jim Rost was a Navy patrol officer on larger, steel-hulled River Assault Group (RAG) craft operated by the Mobile Riverine Forces. Bob Olson was an Army advisor to the Vietnamese working with the Vinh Long Battalion. Each one believed in his mission and what he had been sent to do. These men were not involved in mass troop movements but were alike in that they operated in and with very small units and, in the case of Bob Olson, sometimes worked alone. Because of that and because they died during a time when we were turning the war over to the Vietnamese

("Vietnamization"), they all knew the country and understood the people they were trying to help.

They were not "big-shots" in the sense that they were major policy or decision makers. They were "grunts", doers, implementers, "hands-on" people who were carrying out the decisions of others; but, in the final analysis, they represented what most of war making is all about. They saw war at first-hand and didn't flinch from it. Their names are just three among more than 58,000 on the Vietnam wall. But to their families, those they left behind, they were everything. I have been fortunate to have met with these families and hope that this retelling does justice to the sacrifice that they made when their loved ones were lost in Vietnam. Perhaps others might tell it better, but it is a story that should be told. These three men I knew changed my life for the better. I hope that remembering what they did will help others understand what it was like when, in Vietnam, our nation went to war. To the families of these men, and to the thousands of other families similarly affected, I dedicate this book.

Rolland Kidder

Road Trips

The odyssey began 40 years ago. I was on the back of Thu Trung Van's motorbike heading north on Highway #1 from My Tho in the Mekong Delta toward Saigon; we were on our way to dinner with his family. It was January 1970 and the war was raging all around us. A helicopter air strike was visible to the west and the two-lane road was clogged with jeeps and military vehicles of all kinds.

Today, Thu and I are traveling the same road, but we are on a very different kind of mission.

A Japanese-made SUV carries us south on what is now a four-lane highway lined with factories, commercial shops, and industrial parks. We stop at a fancy restaurant that Thu says is "run by the government." Tourist buses are parked outside. Inside, Australians at the next table are traveling on what brochures call the "three-day Mekong Delta tour."

Amazing: forty years ago, a tour on this stretch of highway meant you were in a war zone. Today, the tour groups are enroute for boat rides on small canals, with a final stop at the floating market in Can Tho. Thu and I, instead, are headed for a small village called Quoi An on the Mang Thit River. It's one of the places that we patrolled during the war.

I have with me a photo from 1969 of an old French church we would like to visit. In the courtyard of this church, the toughest man I ever met killed an enemy soldier using a pop flare as a weapon. War requires some strange and awful actions. Today, it is a place for prayer and worship. That night forty years ago, it was a strategic location, ideal for an ambush.

The road narrows and becomes bumpy as we pass terra-cotta factories and finally arrive at a ferry crossing. Thu negotiates with some shop vendors. Soon, at a rental cost of about $25, we are on a motorized sampan heading downriver. After just a couple of miles, the church comes into view. We scramble ashore.

Thu interprets as we talk with a family that lives next door. The family appears to be poor. Yet, their small house is constructed of masonry, has electricity, and one of the Honda motorbikes ubiquitous to Vietnam is parked outside. One of the sons, in his twenties, has a cell phone; we exchange contact information. He and his family have lived in this place for only five or six years.

The last time I was in front of this old church, we were trying to stop enemy activity along the river. We had been informed that the area around the church had been booby-trapped, and so our naval forces had made no effort to go ashore here. Yet one night, I dropped off Army Captain Robert Olson at this very spot. Olson was a ranger on his second tour of duty. He had been working with a special South Vietnamese army unit trying to pacify the area.

Our boat put Olson ashore just after dark, and by pre-arranged signal, we returned to pick him up at 0300. He had spent the intervening hours squatting near the church, dressed and armed like the enemy—black pajamas and carrying an AK-47. He spoke Vietnamese relatively well. Sometime during the night a guerrilla fighter approached and, assuming Olson was a compatriot, said, "Hello, comrade." Olson responded by killing the man with a hand-held pop flare. We heard no gunfire that night.

I wasn't exactly sure why I wanted to go back to that church, but I sensed it could provide some answers for me or, at least, some peace. Olson was doing vital but gruesome work during the war. I never questioned that. After all, the enemy had taken control of the church and had intended to use it to kill as many of us as possible. I just hoped that four decades later, the church would still stand and have returned to its original purpose.

What relief, then, when the family told us that this small church was in use again. It was served by a priest from a nearby parish. I thought Olson would have appreciated that.

I know many Americans who served in the Vietnam War, but most have chosen not to go back. Out of curiosity, I agreed to make this trip, but it was more than that—I wanted to see for myself what this nation had become after we had left. That story has not been effectively told.

But this journey was only a part of a larger mission, one that should have been undertaken many years before. I wanted to know how the families of three fallen Americans had been affected by their loss. The sad reality was that most of us who served knew someone who didn't come home. Over the years, I've been moved by the memories of three men I knew. I resolved to find their families, wherever they were, and share my remembrances of their loved ones and admiration for them. And I resolved to record their impact on parents, children, and families. This effort took me across the United States and out of the country. What I found humbled me, and I discovered lessons for a nation that still grapples with the effects of the war.

I was forced to revisit some of the worst experiences of my life. Floating down the river today, I see landmarks that stir the memories. We pass a familiar spot that today appears unremarkable. But you do not forget where you were when you found out a friend had died. I still feel like I can see the man we called the "Chief" standing in front of me. The worst part of this experience, this backtracking in time, has been the discovery of details that I had never known.

When the Chief lay mortally wounded, I learned that he had pleaded, "I can't die." I didn't completely understand why this was true until I found his family.

*   *   *

This man, Chief Petty Officer Eldon Tozer, was killed on the Vinh Te Canal. I had made a couple of attempts since the war to communicate with his family but without success. It was time to change that. After several Internet searches and making some long-shot phone calls, I spoke with one of his daughters, Janet Tozer Rasmussen, in central Michigan. I told her that I would soon be driving to a 45th seminary reunion near Chicago.

"On the way back," I asked her, "Could I stop and meet you and talk more about your father and your family?"

"I would enjoy that very much," was her response. My journey, which had begun with a trip to Vietnam, would take on a new dimension.

I planned the road trip. I would drive from my home in western New York out to the Midwest to attend the seminary reunion in Illinois. Then, on the way home, I would drive to Michigan to meet Janet and her sister, Donna. A lot of water had gone over the dam in the past forty-plus years, but I felt ready for the trip and, in my bones, knew it was something that I needed to do. Plus, it had been snowing almost non-stop; I was getting cabin fever and needed a diversion from the weather. So one day in late March, I fired up our snow-savvy, four-wheel-drive Subaru and headed west out through the remnants of New York in the southwestern corner of the state, through the small slice of Pennsylvania near Erie, and into northeastern Ohio and then south out of Cleveland to the Ohio Turnpike.

It was cold, wintry and late in the day as I finally drove west into Indiana. This country was as I had always remembered it. The monotonous, straight Ohio Turnpike morphed seamlessly into the Indiana Toll Road. The snow was gone but there was a bite in the air. Everything seemed brown: the stubble of endless cornfields waiting for spring plowing and one look-a-like farm after another, coming and going as I crossed the invisible state line on the Interstate. The only noticeable difference from my memory four decades old was that the road signs had changed. The state of Indiana no longer operates this highway. It is run by a foreign-owned, Wall Street-created joint venture. The terrain though was the same, just as it was when I was here in 1966.

At the end of my four-year stint in seminary in Illinois, I had gone to work in Indiana, a state of 91 counties . . . and visited every one of them. I worked with a wonderful man, John Mitchell, who was running statewide for the position of Secretary of State. He was a college-educated corn farmer from Shelby County, the first Environmental Commissioner of the state of Indiana, a former state legislator and also a close friend of Senator Birch Bayh from their days at Purdue. John Mitchell was the kind of person everyone hoped would go into politics . . . but 1966 wasn't to be his year. By early October, as you entered these mostly rural counties, there were prominent billboards along the highway, which said flatly: "It's a Republican year!" And so it would be. By the mid-1960's, the country had begun to sour on Lyndon Johnson and the Great Society. President Johnson's promise of "guns and butter"—you can fight a war in Vietnam as well as rescue the nation from poverty—wasn't panning out. People were upset. The human cost of war combined with the financial cost of social programs was not a winning political formula.

John McPhee, when he wrote his book *In Suspect Terrain*, described this part of the country as "the continent's calm, the Stable Interior Craton, where a thin veneer of sediment lies flat upon the stolid fundament." Politically, as well as geologically, the Midwest has always been known as the solid, even-tempered, common sense, unchanging center of America. That was not the case in 1966. Years of tumult over civil rights and now the national debate over the Vietnam War had all come to the heartland, to places like Indiana and Ohio. The break-out of pent-up feelings would occur four years later here on the great "Craton," at Kent State University in Ohio. The 1960's were a topsy-turvy time even in the stable Midwest. Opinions were strong, and divisions were sharp; back then, I was living right in the middle of it.

* * *

It was getting late, I was tired from driving, and it was time for a respite. I pulled off the Interstate at Elkhart, Indiana. When I was in seminary, I would have driven across all of Ohio, Indiana, gone through the time zone change between Indiana and Illinois and then pushed on through Chicago to my suburban destination of Naperville. But not on this night. I felt my seventy years, my back hurt and it was time to stop.

A cheap and clean Day's Inn was waiting, and I pulled into a Texas Road House that had my name written all over it. I went to the bar, ordered a beer and steak sandwich, and immediately started chatting with a salesman from Holland, Michigan. Soon we were talking about everything from healthcare to the war in Libya to what are our kids were doing and where they live. I've always loved this about the Midwest. People come right to the point. There are no pretensions out here. What you see is what you get. The conversation was good, but supper was soon over and I needed to get to bed because I had an early start in the morning. I had a lunch scheduled the next day in Naperville, Illinois—a conversation with an old friend of mine whom I hadn't seen since 1964.

In the morning, I was on the road before dawn, stopped at a drive-through McDonalds, ordered coffee and one of those unhealthy-but-very-tasty breakfast sandwiches that my wife always tells me not to eat, and then drove west on the Interstate heading for Illinois. When I arrived in Naperville, unlike the Indiana Toll Road, it looked nothing like I remember. There were new super highways, development was everywhere, and corporate America had sprung up along I-88, erasing the farm fields that once bordered the town. One of those hotels with the ubiquitous "Inn & Suites" in its name came into view, and I checked in for what I hoped would be a homecoming of sorts with old friends who were fellow seminarians many years ago.

In those days, there was probably no religious denomination more identified with the Midwest than Methodism, and that is what I was studying with the possibility of becoming a Methodist minister. And there was probably no course of study one could have taken in the 1960's more focused on social and political change than biblical theology. America was changing, confronting some of its ancient ghosts from days gone by and, at the local church level, especially in the cities, things were changing. I had grown up on a dairy farm in upstate New York but, for the next four years, I would see things from a very different perspective. The communities and churches of Chicago and its suburbs were caught up in what was becoming known as the Civil Rights Movement, largely led by Christian ministers, including one from Atlanta by the name of Martin Luther King.

My lunch appointment the day I arrived in Naperville was with another Martin, Martin Deppe, a retired Methodist minister from the Chicago area. I hadn't seen him since we, along with a black student from Tougaloo College, had visited an all-white church in Jackson, Mississippi in January, 1964. We were turned away because the Church was segregated and blacks were not allowed to enter. It seemed a small effort at the time, but it was part of a larger movement. We had committed ourselves to helping start a process to break down the racial barriers in the country, at least within the confines of organized Methodism. (It wouldn't be until 1974 that the accepted practice of confining African Americans in a segregated "Central Jurisdiction" would officially be discontinued in the Methodist Church.)

After reliving some of this history over lunch with Martin Deppe, I headed back to the old seminary, and for the next two days visited friends and listened to the reflections of former faculty members about what we had experienced during those heady seminary days of the 1960's. It hit me again of how fortunate I was to have been in this place and how that experience had so changed my own life. As I looked around the old chapel, I also tried to quantify what these seminary friends of mine had accomplished because of it. At the end of four years, I decided not to enter the Christian ministry. Yet most of my fellow seminarians were ordained, became pastors of churches and, in so doing, had helped the world become a better place.

An alumnus who graduated a few years after I did spoke of what it had been like here after the Kent State shootings in 1970. The seminary student body, like the country, had been divided between hawks and doves. There was tension and division at the seminary over the issue of the Vietnam War. The school confronted the issue finally by putting a moratorium on all classes for a week. The chapel was open every day for worship, for talk, for efforts to try to find unity amidst the chaos, for reconciliation to achieve healing where division had sprung out. But, by then, I was completely disconnected from it. My world had entirely changed. I had become directly involved in the war effort. I had gone to Vietnam in the Mekong Delta as a Navy Patrol Officer.

*   *   *

The next morning, after the seminary reunion, I departed Naperville for my meeting in Michigan. It was another cold day as I drove east, out of Illinois, through Indiana and into southern Michigan on I-94. The reunion of the past couple of days had my mind spinning about everything that had happened to me in the 1960's when I was a student. As I crossed the Michigan state line, I stopped for gas and coffee and saw signs to a state park, Warren Dunes. When I was only ten or twelve years old my aunt had taken us to see these magnificent sand dunes on the shore of Lake Michigan, and I decided to visit them again.

The entrance to the state park was deserted. Apparently, there are no toll takers or ticket dispensers on cold, windy days in March at state parks in Michigan. I drove in and the parking lot was empty. The wind was drifting the sand and blowing it like the sheets of snow that we see all winter in upstate New York. Was this happenstance? I felt right then that my life was like drifting sand. Things had moved around a lot in the past forty years, and I was headed that day toward an unknown ending—I was scheduled to have lunch with two daughters of my old friend from Vietnam. It had taken me a long time to track them down.

After his death, Eldon Tozer's kids had been raised by relatives, the family had moved around a lot, and last names had changed because of weddings and marriages. He was the father of four children (three girls and a boy). Finally, through the magic of Internet search engines, I had been able to locate two of his daughters. I had never promised my Navy friend that I would try and see his kids if he were killed in the war, but, after his death, I had made a promise to myself that someday I would try to follow through and speak with them about their dad.

It was an obligation that I hoped to finally fulfill later that day.

In the Warren Dunes State Park, it was so chilly and windy that I decided not to get out and walk but, instead, looked at the dunes and Lake Michigan from inside the car. It looked like the same place we visited with my aunt many years ago. Now I was alone. There were no other cars around.

Sometimes I think better when I write, so I pulled out a pen and made some notes for the upcoming meeting. How should I greet Eldon Tozer's daughters? What facts about their father are they going to be interested in? Was there any insight that I can give them about him, about the war, about what the Navy was doing in the Mekong Delta in this war? Their father had actually been a Canadian but he was serving in the U.S. Navy. How had that happened? Back in those days when Canada was mentioned, it was generally about young American men avoiding the draft by moving to Canada. What had compelled their father to leave Canada, join the U.S. Navy and go to Vietnam?

And perhaps of greatest interest, what had happened to them after he was killed?

The questions in my mind seemed endless, but I also realized I was stalling. There was trepidation heading into this meeting. I didn't know how it would or should go. But if I was going to make lunch, I needed to get going. I put the pen down, drove out of the state park and headed north and east, up the Interstate.

*   *   *

When you arrive in Ionia, Michigan, it happens rather abruptly. The land around is as flat as a pancake and the two-lane highway looks like the entrance to many small towns. You first see signs indicating that a community is up ahead and then the outlines of 21ˢᵗ century America begin to appear—the fast food restaurants, gas stations and then the inevitable big box stores. I was worried that maybe I had missed the town because suddenly the strip development ended, the parking lots and stores disappeared, and the road quickly descended. At the bottom of the hill there was a broad, beautiful valley, then a bridge appeared spanning the Grand River. Beyond that, I could see the makings of a small town—church steeples, a business district and a traffic light. Ionia was still ahead. I drove to the light and turned right on Main Street. It was apparent that the town fathers had been investing in this old downtown area. There was a new brick street and the facades of buildings had been spruced up. Then I saw the sign.

When I had spoken with Janet about getting together with her and her sister, she had suggested we meet at her sister's restaurant. "By the way," she said with great pride, "you might be interested in its name. It's named after our father. It's called Eldon's Café."

This was the man we both had known. Her father and my friend:

> Chief Petty Officer Eldon W. Tozer
> Born: March 29, 1934
> Killed: November 20, 1969
> Buried: Town Cemetery, Cullens Brook, Quebec
> Name inscribed: Vietnam Wall, Washington, D.C. Panel 16W Line 103

One

The Chief's Family

I thought I was prepared to learn about what happened to Chief Tozer's family. I was wrong.

I had spoken with Janet Tozer Rasmussen on the phone and recognized her voice when she met me at the door of the café. Her sister, Donna, was inside waiting on tables and greeted us as we came in. On the wall, to the left of the door, was a framed photo of their father, Eldon W. Tozer; and below it, was a description of his military service with a special welcome to veterans who come to the restaurant. We sat down to talk. It was time for me to more fully explain my connection to their father.

"There were others who knew him better than I did," I said. "Your father was a Chief Petty Officer, and was revered by those who knew him. Because he was an enlisted man and had risen through the ranks, he had a special relationship with the boat crews, most of whom were younger and of lower rank. I would describe him as quiet, competent and effective. His job was the same as mine—a patrol officer on boats called PBR's (Patrol Boat River). In the Navy, making Chief, as a non-commissioned officer, was a badge of honor. I called him 'Chief'; the men did, too. To us, he was Chief Tozer. He had earned his stripes."

"We got to know each other by working together on patrols, especially in our operations along the Cambodian border where we would operate for several days at a time from a remote base camp on the Vinh Te Canal. There was a strong camaraderie. Back at our main supply base on the Mekong River, we lived a more typical Navy life with separate berthing and messing facilities for officers, chiefs, and enlisted men. But out on patrol, we were all together, dependent upon each other and close to each other. Rank meant very little in those circumstances."

It was in that setting that I had gotten to know and appreciate their father, Chief Eldon Tozer.

It wasn't long before the sisters began to talk about their own memories of their father. "I was nine and Donna was seven when he was killed," Janet explained, "and so I remember more than the younger kids. My brother, David, Donna's twin, was also seven and my sister, Gwen, was only four. I remember my Dad as a quiet person but one who could still draw a crowd. I still recall his love for fishing. When we lived in Massachusetts, he'd go fishing with my uncles or some friends, and I remember him coming back with lots of salmon. Those were good times!"

But our conversation soon turned to other memories which were not as good. Chief Tozer had gone home on emergency leave from Vietnam in September, 1969 because his wife had been killed in an automobile accident in San Diego. "The night that happened," Janet explained, "we were being taken care of by a baby sitter, and my Mom didn't come home. When my Mom was killed, I was told that they initially had difficulty identifying her body. The babysitter hadn't heard anything and didn't know what to do, so she called the police. The police came and took us to what must have been some kind of a juvenile detention facility. I was scared to death. I didn't know why we were there. Everybody kept asking, 'Who's your Dad, who's your Dad?' I remember being in a little office and being all upset because my brother and sisters had been taken and put in a different part of the facility. Donna says that the only thing she remembers about the experience is being on the other side of a chain link fence from me, and we were crying as we held hands through the fence.

"We were there for at least three or four days," she continued, "and I didn't know much of anything until my Dad came walking in, in his uniform. He came in with my Uncle Bill and my Uncle Jerry. I'll never forget that moment. We just went running for him yelling, 'Dad, Dad!'

"I still didn't know that my mother had died. My Dad got us out of that place and took us back home where other family members were gathered. My Aunt Ruth and Aunt Frances were there, along with Uncle Bill and Uncle Jerry, but my Mom wasn't there, and that is when they told us. They tried to make us feel better so they took us to the zoo, but I was sick, running a high temperature, so we soon had to go home. I remember that night, my Dad carrying me to my room and saying that Mom had gone to heaven. That's what he told me. He also told me that we would be going to live with Uncle Bill and our four cousins in Oklahoma, and that we would stay there for a while because he was going back to the boat. 'Janet, honey,' he said, 'I will come home and we will find a place to live.' I remember this clearly and I was only nine years old."

I tried to absorb the memories. Nine years old. She paused, then continued.

"He came back with us to Oklahoma and my last memory of him, after he said 'goodbye' to us for the final time, was his getting on a plane in his dress uniform. After my Dad left, we kept waiting for him to return. It seemed like forever. We began to get ready for Thanksgiving, and Christmas was ahead, and after that we knew he would be coming home."

Chief Tozer never did come home. I felt the weight of her words as she recalled the loss; just months after her mother had died.

"The day they told me he had died, I was in complete denial. I don't know how I stayed together or how the family kept me together. Uncle Bill came to our school and took the three of us who were there out of class in order to tell us. He had tears in his eyes when he picked us up at school. His own kids were not in the car, so I thought that maybe we had been taken out of school because we had done something wrong. He didn't speak on the way home. When we got home the relatives were there again, just like when Mom had died, and you'd think I could have put two and two together and have figured out that it was bad news again . . . but I didn't. Then Uncle Bill took me for the walk. He held my hand, then picked me up and said, 'Janet I have something to tell you.' Then he told me my Dad had died. I don't remember anything about what happened that day after that."

When Janet finished this story, I felt numb. All of my own experiences in Vietnam, all of the books I have read about it, all of the controversy of the war, all seemed to pale before the story of this family. Their mother had been killed in September 1969; and their father was killed in Vietnam two months later. A father went off to war, came back for his wife's funeral, left his children with relatives to return to Vietnam only to be killed himself. Could there be anything more sad? Four children were now on their own with both parents gone.

It didn't end there for these four kids. Within a year, Janet's Uncle Bill took her on another walk, this time to tell her that he and his wife were divorcing. He told Janet that he just couldn't afford to raise eight children, his own four and the four Tozer siblings. In this situation, his only option was to send his brother-in-law's children to an orphanage in Oklahoma. Though they were not separated this time, it was another bad experience for Chief Tozer's kids, and they longed to leave. After about a year in the orphanage, their mother's sister, Aunt Bea, came and took them to her home in the Grand Rapids area of Michigan where they were able to make a new start. Bea and her husband, Frank, a World War II veteran, had already raised their own family; they now took on the task of raising three nieces and a nephew. "They were wonderful to us," Janet said, "and we soon were calling them 'Mom' and 'Dad'. They are both gone now, but we had a good upbringing once we got to Michigan and started living with them."

* * *

When Americans think of war, we usually think of precise dates of when war begins and ends. The Revolutionary War for us starts at Lexington and Concord and ends at Yorktown. The bombardment of Fort Sumter we see as the beginning of the Civil War and Appomattox as its end. In the twentieth century, Pearl Harbor marked for us the beginning of World War II and VE Day (Victory in Europe) and VJ Day (Victory over Japan) marked its end. Such precision was not the case with the Vietnam War. It was a war that we sort of slid into over time and then slowly extricated ourselves from as public support of the effort slipped away. An incident in the Bay of Tonkin prompted President Lyndon Johnson to ramp up the war in 1964, but actually the number of American military and civilian personnel in Vietnam had been growing steadily since at least 1962. According to the Paris Peace Accords, the war officially ended on January 27, 1973. Yet, as chronicled on the Vietnam Wall, the war is given a starting point of June 8, 1956 as the date of its first casualty; the last American name engraved on the Wall died May 15, 1975. For most of us affected by the Vietnam War, it started and ended with our own involvement. The war, for me, really started when I went in country (as we called it then) in July 1969, and it ended when I came home in June 1970. For Thu Trung Van, who would go back to Vietnam with me more than 40 years later, the war started when he joined the Vietnamese Navy in April 1964. It ended when he fled the country with his family on April 29, 1975, the day that the Communist north took control in South Vietnam.

For Donna and Janet Tozer and their brother and sister, the war started the day that their Father went to Vietnam; it ended when his body came back. But as I conversed with these two women, it was apparent that, in their lives, the impact of that war had never really ended. Soon into our meeting at Eldon's Café, it was clear that their world as young children was forever transformed by this war. As Janet and I talked over lunch, Donna supervised the kitchen and helped wait on tables. It was a busy day; many people came in for some hot soup and a sandwich. As lunch hour faded into mid-afternoon, business slowed down and Donna was able to join in the conversation. She wanted to know more about her Dad, what he was doing in Vietnam, and what his job was like being a Patrol Officer in the Mekong Delta.

I had my computer with me and plugged it in to show them some slides. Some were from our Navy days in 1969 and others from my recent trip back to Vietnam. They seemed to appreciate the description of events back then and what it is like today. Periodically, they asked questions about what his duties were; they were particularly interested in our operations along the Cambodian border on the Vinh Te Canal where their father was killed. It was a time of reflection for them and for me. I felt good about having come to this small town in rural Michigan to meet two of Chief Tozer's children. As we finished our conversation, we talked about the Tozer side of the family. I explained that it was through a conversation with their father's sister (their aunt), Frances Tozer Gregoire, who lives in New Brunswick, Canada that I had found out about their being raised near Grand Rapids. Frances did not have their addresses or phone numbers, but it was my phone call with her that started my search for them. Through one of the "people search" programs available on the Internet I had found the name Janet (Tozer) Rasmussen.

It had been a long time since either Janet or Donna had seen or spoken with the Tozers of New Brunswick and Quebec, but they both expressed interest in reopening communications and wrote down their Aunt Frances' phone number. As I got ready to leave, I mentioned that it was still on my list to try and visit their Aunt Frances and to visit their father's grave. "We would like to do that as well," Janet said. "When my husband retires next year, we'll have a little more time and money to travel. I hope that we can get up there to see them. Please, if you talk to Aunt Frances, say hello from us and give her our best."

We embraced each other and had our picture taken outside on the sidewalk in front of Eldon's Café. It had been an intense two-hours. There was so much to talk about, so much pent-up emotion and so many heart-rending remembrances of times long past. It was difficult to end our conversation and to say goodbye, but it was time to go.

Janet and Donna came to wave to me as I got into the car to continue my trip.

As I left town, reversed track and crossed the Grand River Valley heading south, I felt a renewed commitment in my gut that I should stop and pay my respects to Eldon Tozer's family in Canada. There were also the families of two other men I knew who didn't make it home: Bob Olson, an Army Captain, and Jim Rost, a Navy LTJG. I felt a renewed and gnawing obligation, now forty years old, that I should try to reach out to their families as well. My visit back to Vietnam had been fulfilling, but this meeting at Eldon's Café was cathartic. I sensed, also, that it was appreciated and meaningful for Chief Tozer's two daughters. There can probably never be total closure for those who have lost loved ones on the battlefield, but the recognition of old friendships, the reliving of memories, the recollection of the vitality and strength of those who died—can have its own healing power.

Eldon Tozer, Jim Rost and Bob Olson, I am sure, did not share all of my views on the war, nor did we have all of the same tasks. However, we operated on the same rivers, we saw the same country, and we shared a common experience. Maybe knowing more about these experiences will give their families and mine an understanding of what we were doing and help them make sense of what Vietnam was all about.

I had closed the loop with at least part of Chief Tozer's family. Thinking of Eldon, Bob and Jim—I knew there was more to be done. First, I would go to Canada in search of more answers. It wasn't a great war, but it was our war, and what happened there should not be forgotten.

ELDON TOZER AS A YOUNG SEAMAN APPRENTICE

ELDON TOZER AND HIS WIFE, GWENDOLYN

**DAUGHTERS DONNA AND JANET AT
ELDON'S CAFÉ, IONIA, MICHIGAN**

THE TOZER CHILDREN—GWEN, DAVID, DONNA & JANET

THE WHITE HOUSE
WASHINGTON

December 3, 1969

Dear Janet, David, Donna and Gwendal:

I have learned with great sorrow of the death of your
father, Chief Petty Officer Eldon W. Tozer.

There is little I could say, I know, that would make
your grief any less. I can only assure you that the
nation he died to serve shares your grief, and will
forever honor his memory.

I pray for the day when this war can be ended, and
peace restored. I wish that your father could have
lived to see that day. His courage, his devotion
and his sacrifice have brought it closer. When it
comes, there will be a special place in the thoughts
of his countrymen for him, and for you, and for the
others who have borne the burdens of loss.

Mrs. Nixon joins me in extending our deepest
sympathy and in the hope that the profound respect
your father has so tragically earned will help sustain
and comfort you. You will be in our prayers, and in
our hearts.

Sincerely,

Richard Nixon

Two

A Sister

When I walked into Frances Tozer's apartment in Campbellton, New Brunswick, I sensed an immediate recognition—though we had never met before. We had spoken on the phone so maybe it was just voice familiarity, but I felt that somehow we knew each other, like two friends who hadn't seen each other for a long time. Her mannerisms reminded me of Eldon and I could see glimpses of him in her face.

We didn't take time for introductions but began talking of him, her memories of him, and what it had been like growing up in the Tozer family in nearby Quebec. She is now Frances Tozer Gregoire but her husband is no longer living. Her only son, Eldon, died two years ago in a tragic accident while driving a four-wheel-drive ATV on a trip with friends in the Quebec woods, and her brother, Winston, died unexpectedly within the last six months. She was obviously lonely and felt the sadness of these recent events, but she was also still affected by vivid memories of the tragic death of her brother, Eldon, more than forty years ago.

"I have had a lot of sadness in my life," she said.

I mentioned to her that back in my Vietnam days with Eldon, I was unaware that he was a Canadian. He had no Canadian expressions that I can remember, such as pronouncing "schedule" with an "sh" sound, or making the word "out" sound like "aut".

I knew him as an American and it was a surprise to me when I found out that he had been buried in Quebec as a Canadian citizen.

"It was a surprise to us, as well, when he joined the U.S. Navy," Frances explained. "My father had wanted him to come back and become part of the small saw mill business that he owned. Eldon had moved to Massachusetts to find work, and was living there with my sister Mona when he decided to join the Navy. He told us that he had been advised by the immigration service that if he did not submit himself to the U.S. military draft, he would be sent back to Canada. He decided, instead, to join the U.S. Navy so he could stay in America. We have a history in the Tozer family of our ancestors being seafarers, so he must have chosen the Navy over being drafted into the Army."

Though we haven't had a military draft in the United States since 1973, the Selective Service System still requires that: "If you are a man ages 18 through 25 and living in the U.S., then you must register with Selective Service." Frances' remarks were a reminder of what it was like being a male over the age of 18 and living in the United States from the World War II era through the end of the Vietnam War when that policy was in force. We were all subject to the draft and required to register with the local Draft Board. I had forgotten that foreign nationals permanently working in the United States were also subject to the draft. That is what had apparently prompted Eldon Tozer, in 1958, to join the U.S. Navy. Interestingly, it had also prompted me to do the same. In 1966, after graduating from seminary, I lost my student deferment and expected that soon I would be hearing from the local Draft Board. Rather than join the Army or be drafted, I chose the Navy. We had joined the Navy at different times but probably for similar reasons.

* * *

As I look back on those days of the draft, in a way I yearn for them. We all complained about the draft, about how it was a pain having to think about joining the military. But to us, that obligation was a part of life. We had never known anything but the draft. We grew up talking with our fathers and their friends about World War II; they had all been subject to the draft. We knew many men who had served during the Korean War and others who had served in Europe in the military during that time; they all had lived with the reality of the draft. It wasn't a matter of choice, it was a matter of fact: if you were male and over the age of 18, you were probably going to serve in the military, either voluntarily or involuntarily. That meant that not only were you going to be affected or inconvenienced by the draft, but so would your family. Mothers would worry, and sisters would become concerned about whether their boyfriends or fiancés would be home to be married. Fathers were just prosaic about it; they had been subject to the draft and going into the military was something their sons were expected to do.

How different that is from today.

Now we go to war and nobody worries about it. You go into the military only if you choose to and then, it is just that—your choice. There is no longer a sense of common sacrifice. True, we do stand up and cheer the troops at football games, and everyone quiets down when names are read of those who aren't coming home, but the gut feeling, the implicit recognition by everyone that a military obligation is a joint and common enterprise, is gone. I have become more anti-war as I have grown older. War usually solves so little and yet costs so much. I have also become more concerned about the selective attitude we take as citizens that somehow we can buy our way in and out of foreign military involvement without asking for common sacrifice and that we can do it using borrowed money. It is more than the borrowing of the money. We are somehow borrowing, leasing or loaning out our civic obligation in the process. Our old enemy from World War II, Germany, until recently, required universal service from its citizens. Countries living in a continual war zone, like Israel, require it. The United States of America, the leader of the free world, takes a pass on universal military service. Our wars are now fought by a military class that has chosen the vocation, not by civilians who are subject to its vagaries. As one of my Vietnam veteran friends put it: "During the Iraq and Afghanistan wars, the military went to war. The rest of us went to the mall."

My musing about all of this, of course, is not why I was in Canada speaking with Eldon Tozer's sister. Yet, in an unforeseen kind of way, it was the concept of common sacrifice, as codified in the universal draft that we knew in the 1950's and 1960's, which led her brother and me to join the U.S. Navy. He came to like the Navy and ultimately decided to make it a career. I was a Naval Reserve Officer and spent only 3 ½ years on active duty. However, while we were in Vietnam, we were in the same boat, so to speak: both of us implementing the foreign policy decisions of the United States, both taking the risks associated with that, both paying our taxes, both taking a little piece of that shared sacrifice that we assumed came with being good citizens. Will we ever get back to that? There would probably be fewer wars or, at least, those who decide to fight them would be more concerned about what war means, if everyone were involved in the execution of it, either directly or indirectly.

*   *   *

A couple of friends, brothers Gale and Bob, had helped me make the drive to Canada, and now they were waiting down in the car for Frances and me. It was time to get going. It had been a thousand-mile drive to get here, to the Gaspe Peninsula. Yesterday, we had driven 15 hours to Caribou, Maine. That morning, we had traveled another three hours north into New Brunswick. The rest of the day was going to be spent traveling across the border to Quebec and along the shores of the Bay of Chaleur with our ultimate destination being Cullen's Brook and a cemetery where Eldon Tozer is buried. I knew that it would be an intense day for both Frances and me. Along the way, we were scheduled to stop at New Richmond, Quebec. There, in a small military museum, was an exhibit featuring her brother, with photos from the Vietnam War, write-ups from his funeral, and a display of one of his Navy uniforms and medals. There was much to talk about, much to discover.

As soon as we left Campbellton we crossed a bridge spanning the river that separates New Brunswick from Quebec. There were rolling hills and the road hugged the shore of the bay. I asked Frances about being raised in French-speaking Canada.

"I grew up in Cullen's Brook, a small English community in Quebec," she said. "We were on the eastern side of the Bonaventure River and the French were on the other side. It was a wonderful place to grow up, but we were quite isolated. We had separate schools. Our father spoke French as well as he spoke English, and he managed the Bonaventure Salmon Club for which he received a year-round salary. Most of his employees were French. This fishing and hunting club included many prominent Canadians, including Steve Molson of the famous beer-making family. French-speaking people were all around us, but our family came from English roots.

"I wish that I were bilingual," she continued, "but my parents would not let the girls in the family mix with the

16

French-speaking community. I guess they were afraid that we would get in trouble with the French boys. But Eldon and Winston, the boys in our family, were allowed to have friends in the French community. So they both grew up being bilingual."

I mentioned to Frances that perhaps, though I have no documentation for it, this language skill might have helped Eldon in Vietnam. As a former colony of France, many Vietnamese spoke French better than English. It is quite possible that in dealing with the Vietnamese we were training, Chief Tozer could have used his French speaking skills.

As we drove along, Frances talked about the wonderful memories of her brother. "Everyone loved Eldon," she explained, "and he was a real favorite in our family. I recall competing with my sister for the job of babysitting him when he was little. We all wanted to protect him and help him. He made friends easily and so many people were disappointed when he decided to stay in the United States and not come home. The last time he did come home, after the death of his wife, he walked on the beach, right near here. He loved the sea and he loved this place. I always thought that someday he would come back and settle here."

Though it was overcast as we drove, one could see how a person growing up here would want to come back, especially if he liked the outdoors. The homes were small, but clean and well kept. The air was pure and the ocean vista was continually in front of us. The churches here are also unique; most are Roman Catholic reflecting the French-speaking populace. In every town, a towering church steeple reached up to dominate the skyline for miles around. The steeples looked as if they were made from aluminum or were painted that color.

We stopped to take a photo of the church in Bonaventure, the largest town near Cullen's Brook.

"When Eldon died," Frances told us, "the church offered its sanctuary as the place for the funeral. He had actually been raised in the Anglican Church but it was smaller, and we thought that perhaps a larger building would be needed. It was wonderful when the local priest suggested that the Catholic Church be used for his service—over 500 people came that day. It was also symbolic of how well liked Eldon had been in both the English and French-speaking communities."

We stopped in Bonaventure to visit Frances' niece, Debbie. Her father, Winston, Eldon's and Frances' brother, had recently died and is also buried at the Cullen's Brook Cemetery. Cullen's Brook is only about five miles from Bonaventure, and Debbie joined us as we drove to the cemetery. Eldon Tozer and Winston Tozer are buried next to each other here on the Tozer family plot.

In the afternoon, after lunch and our visit to the cemetery, we started our drive back toward New Brunswick. Frances had called ahead to let the curator of the War Museum at New Richmond know of our pending arrival, and he was waiting. He was a veteran of World War II, a POW who spent most of the war in Hong Kong incarcerated by the Japanese. It was really quite incredible what he and this small community had done in creating this museum. There were exhibits from all of the wars Canadians had been involved in, and there was one about a war in which they were not directly engaged: Vietnam.

That exhibit was all about Eldon Tozer.

There were photos of him and his family, copies of newspaper articles about his record of service in the U.S. Navy and, of course, newspaper stories about his funeral in 1969. Impressive also was the display of one of his naval uniforms. Canada was not a formal participant in the Vietnam War, but they are proud here in the Gaspe that one of their sons served there in the U.S. Navy.

As we were finishing our museum tour, Steve Tozer arrived—Frances' nephew, son of Winston Tozer. He had been supervising a highway construction job nearby and wanted to stop and thank me for coming to visit his uncle's gravesite. "It honors us that you have come," he said. "I didn't know my Uncle Eldon, but I always knew about him and what he meant to our family. It was a great loss for my aunt, my father and for the whole family when he was killed in Vietnam. Thank you for coming."

His words left me momentarily speechless. I tried to explain, though poorly, that thanks were not necessary, that my visit was something that I needed and wanted to do, that I too, along with all the Navy men who knew Chief Tozer, had great respect for him, that it was a great loss for us as well when he died, and that . . .

I'm not sure all that I did say, but it was a powerful ending to a very emotional day.

We took a photo standing in front of the museum and said our goodbyes. It was time to take Frances back to her home in Campbellton. I had met two of Chief Tozer's daughters in Michigan and now I had met his sister and some of his family in Canada. If my own father were still alive and had he been on this trip, I believe he would have said, in his own simple, common sense way, what I was thinking as we drove south out of Canada toward home: Eldon Tozer had come from "good stock," and he had left behind a loving family. It was a family that had suffered, and persevered.

**BONAVENTURE ROMAN CATHOLIC CHURCH,
BONAVENTURE, QUEBEC**

**AUTHOR WITH FRANCES TOZER, ELDON TOZER'S
SISTER, AT THE BAY OF CHALEUR, GASPÉ, QUEBEC**

**BUTCH JARVINEN AND ELDON TOZER, VIETNAM 1969
(PHOTO IN WAR MUSEUM, NEW RICHMOND, QUEBEC)**

Three

Training

For Vietnam Navy veterans, a "PBR" described both a drink and a boat. While a Pabst Blue Ribbon beer could be consumed on occasion in the Mekong Delta, for us, a PBR usually meant "Patrol Boat River", the 32 ft. fiberglass boat which was the fighting platform from which we operated.

But, before we were sent to the PBRs on the rivers of Vietnam, we had to be trained, and there was one training exercise in particular that none of us looked forward to.

It was a total immersion experience that most PBR sailors will remember forever—the one-week survival school at Whidbey Island, Washington, on Puget Sound. This was as real as role-playing could be. Since the Korean War, the military had been concerned that soldiers, sailors and airmen needed better training in survival techniques and, especially, in surviving in a prisoner-of-war camp. For six days at Whidbey Island, we were given daily classes in survival, what to eat and how to live off the land. We were given water but no food. We tried to collect clams along the shore, trap rabbits and even boil grass for soup, but the pickings were slim. By the sixth day we were starving, and it is amazing to see what happens to men who starve. For the first time in my Navy life, the number one topic among the men turned from girls and sex to . . . food! We knew that we would be getting food in one more day, but that didn't matter—the craving and the need for food was overpowering. Obviously, the Navy wanted us to have this experience because you see a different side of humanity when people are hungry.

This was also the time when we received training in first aid and in treating those wounded in combat. I remember sitting through films watching medics treating shrapnel wounds, sucking chest wounds, and gunshot wounds. It wasn't pretty, but you paid attention. It was the only formal medical training that we had, and it came to good use in Vietnam.

At the end of the sixth day in survival camp, we were taken in trucks out to the perimeter of the camp area and told that we had three hours to try to remain undetected as we worked our way with compasses back in the direction of the camp. If we arrived undetected, we would get an apple for our efforts! At the end of three hours, a whistle blew telling us this exercise was over and, of course, most of us had been captured, and no one got an apple. It was then that we were taken to the POW camp we had not seen before, but which was located nearby. We would be prisoners for 24 hours. The camp was surrounded by a wall, twenty feet high, covered with barbed wire. Three or four watchtowers topped by machine guns stood at the corners of this fence. The "enemy" was everywhere with red stars on their caps and helmets.

Then the hazing began.

Men were pummeled. Heads were held under water. I was put in a hot box where I squatted for nearly four hours. We had been briefed on a ficticious mission, and it was never to be revealed to the "enemy". Two men broke down under interrogation and revealed the mission anyway. As officers were isolated and taken out of the compound, it was the obligation of the next highest in the chain of command to take charge of the remaining troops in the camp. An analysis of POW camps in the Korean War had shown that camp discipline had broken down when there was no chain of command. Everyone in this camp knew who came next in the chain. Jim Roper, a Lieutenant, was the senior officer in the camp. As a LTJG (Lieutenant Junior Grade), I was #2, and it went on down the line from there. So many of us were taken out for interrogations by the camp guards that, at the end, a Third Class Petty Officer became the camp commander. Through all of this, the chain of command was never broken. The most senior officer or petty officer remained in charge of the prisoners in the compound.

It is hard to describe the reality of this experience. When I had been in charge of the camp, I had negotiated from the "enemy" some food for the troops. We had boiled water on an open fire and put in some oatmeal to cook. We were starved and needed to eat. Just as we got ready to feed the men, a guard came over and kicked the oatmeal into the fire. By the end of 24 hours of this POW camp, combined with a week of not eating, though your head told you that they were just a bunch of Navy trainers masquerading as the enemy, you had become convinced that these guards really were the bad guys.

The way it ended will forever be in my memory. The officers had been brought back into the camp, Jim Roper was again in command, and we had been ordered to march in single file in a circle with bags over our heads. We were stumbling around the camp, exhausted and miserable, with one arm hanging on to the shoulder of the guy in front of us. Then we were told to kneel on the ground. You could almost sense that an execution squad was next. At that moment, over a loudspeaker, we heard The Star Spangled Banner being played. Jim Roper, our commander, yelled: "Everybody up! Nobody kneels when our national anthem is played!" We staggered to our feet. One of the "enemy" ordered us to remove the bags from our heads and there, just as the sun was coming up over Whidbey Island, above the barbed wire and the guard towers, flew the American flag. There wasn't a dry eye in the place. The ordeal was over.

Lt. Roper ordered us to march in columns of four. We tried to keep in step and marched out of that place, as hungry as bears, with tears streaming down our cheeks singing the Marine Hymn: "From the halls of Montezuma to the shores of Tripoli." We were heading for food and were now qualified to go to Vietnam. That experience, like no other I have had before or since, forged a camaraderie that would help carry us through what was to come.

The PBR was the common connection for Eldon Tozer and all who served in U.S. Navy River Divisions in Vietnam. Our first introduction to it was at a training facility at Mare Island, a Naval base near Vallejo, California, in the northeastern corner of San Francisco Bay. Mare Island was a Navy shipyard, and it was also located near the outlet of the Sacramento River, where it enters San Francisco Bay. The Navy had concluded that the delta of the Sacramento River was probably as close to what the Mekong Delta would be like as any place in America. The river there ran backwards when the tide was coming in, and the fingers of the river ran in all directions, similar to the waterways of South Vietnam. The Sacramento River Delta was also a relatively deserted area with only a few farms located along its northern border. It was a place where you could test out the shallow draft of the PBR (only 8-12 inches when the boat was at full speed or "on step"). You could run aground on shallow mud and gravel bars. At high tide, you could glide over these same areas at a top speed of 32 knots. I recall one morning as the sun was coming up, taking a boat with the throttles wide open to the end of one of these fingers of the Sacramento River while it was at high tide, speeding across the end of a flooded pasture, and coming back between the banks of the river a few hundred yards later. This was an amazing boat!

Another attribute of the PBR was its maneuverability. The boat was powered by two 250-horsepower GM diesel engines that were connected to two Jacuzzi pumps. The propulsion system made the PBR, in essence, a jet boat. It was the jets of water shooting out the back that made them go fast but also gave them their maneuverability. If you whirled the steering column when the boat was at full speed, the bow of the boat would dip in the direction of the turn, actually catch in the water like a keel and then "flip" . . . the whole boat would reverse, the stern would almost flip over the bow, and you would be going in the opposite direction. Everyone had to hang on during this maneuver or you would be thrown over the side. The same immediate effect took place with braking action. When you reversed thrust, gates would drop, reversing the jet streams of water and the boat could nearly stop in its 32-foot length. This was a vessel engineered to move quickly in shallow water. Its defense was the same as its offense—speed and maneuverability.

For a small boat, the PBR also had a significant amount of firepower. A rotating tub-type gun mount was located in the bow, where one man operated a twin .50 caliber machine gun. The boat also had the capability of firing either a .50 caliber machine gun or a 60 mm mortar from the stern. When operated on smaller canals, the boat's radar antenna over the canopy could also be removed and replaced with an M-60 machine gun. The placement of this gun at the top of the boat's superstructure improved our ability to shoot over river or canal banks during times of low water. Some PBRs also had a mounted, automatic grenade launcher that could be operated from the side of the vessel.

In short, the Patrol Boat River was a mean, powerful and effective firing platform. (This was the case, of course, as long as the platform itself stayed afloat and maintained its power and speed.) In Vietnam, crewmen would sometimes paint slogans on the forward gun scatter shield. I remember one sign which bluntly said, "The Judge, the Jury and the Executioner," a succinct commentary on what the enemy could expect on the receiving side of these weapons. These small boats were not a welcome sight to the Viet Cong and North Vietnamese who were trying to use the waterways of South Vietnam to their own advantage.

Usually, a crew of four manned each boat: the boat captain, a gunner, an engineman and a seaman who also functioned as a gunner. For safety and mutual fire support, the boats were operated in pairs with a Patrol Officer who was responsible for commanding these two-boat units. Boat captains were usually senior Petty Officers, and Patrol Officers were either commissioned officers (like myself) or Chief Petty Officers, as was the case with Chief Tozer. In addition to the basic four-man crews, once we arrived in Vietnam, each boat, for training purposes, usually carried an additional Vietnamese crewman. In the case of Patrol Officers, there was often a Vietnamese Naval officer onboard.

The training at Mare Island took eight weeks. Days were full of lectures on patrol boat tactics, the capabilities of the PBR, and familiarization of how the boats operated in Vietnam. A couple of times a week, we would take the boats down San Francisco Bay, cross under the big Interstate highway bridge and then proceed up into the sloughs (the fingers) of the Sacramento River. It was always quite a sight along the way to pass what seemed like hundreds of old Navy ships from World War II, now moth-balled, tied up and rusting away. They dwarfed these small, 32-foot fiberglass boats, and reminded us of the incredible effort expended by our nation in winning World War II.

Near the end of our training at Mare Island, we spent an overnight at a mock base camp that had been constructed in the heart of the Sacramento River Delta. The Navy had strung barbed wire, put up some lookout towers, and had done a good job of giving us an idea of what a base camp in Vietnam would look like. We were told that we could expect our base camp to be attacked and our job was to protect it. Of course, that is exactly what happened when one night we were "attacked" by Navy personnel firing blanks and role-playing as Viet Cong or North Vietnamese combatants. Needless to say, the exercise was structured so that we (the trainees) would lose. And we did, but it was a valuable training experience. When we got to Vietnam, many of us would operate either from or in conjunction with base camps that were located on the smaller rivers and canals of the Mekong Delta. It was a good reminder that we were preparing for combat, not for a picnic.

There was also a firing range in a remote area of San Francisco Bay where we could fire M-16s and our machine guns. My most memorable experience in weapons training, however, was a trip we took to Camp Roberts, an Army base in central California. There we learned how to fire mortars and call in artillery. We were taught how to read grid-line maps and walk an artillery barrage toward a target. There were a couple of battered tanks in the valley at Camp Roberts that had probably been used for this kind of target training by hundreds of men headed for Vietnam. When you fired the artillery, you could almost see the artillery shells as they sped toward these targets two or three miles away. In retrospect, the one area of fire support that was probably most important—helicopters and aircraft—would be something that we would not learn until we got to Vietnam.

Of course, the training for Vietnam was not all just learning the business of war; we also got to know each other and had some good times. For these eight weeks, a few us had been housed at a hotel in downtown Vallejo. There had not been enough housing for all of the trainees at Mare Island, so the Navy had rented rooms for us off base. We would gather at the hotel for dinner and drinks and sometimes we'd head out to a bar or nightclub. Inevitably, at some time during the evening, Jim Roper would cheer us up by toasting the "the river of no return." We would laugh, and then drink to what we believed to be the best PBR class ever to have gone through the school.

Because of the nature of our PBR training, the typical separation between officers and enlisted men began to evaporate. That was good because it would be like that in Vietnam when we would operate independently in small groups on boat patrols. I recall one very interesting weekend, near the end of PBR School, which started and ended at the Hotel Vallejo. One of the Petty Officers we hung around with was William Seaman. (How could you not remember such a surname in the Navy?) He had come to me and to a couple of others on a Friday afternoon, and we each loaned him $50 for a small nest egg so that he could take the bus to Reno and gamble at the casino. We joked over the weekend that we would never see that money again. Then, on Sunday night, Seaman drove up in a taxi with Nevada plates, came into the bar of the hotel with two big stacks of money and ordered everyone a drink—he had won $180,000 in Reno! It was unbelievable and we all celebrated. At the end of the evening, Jim Roper bought a bottle of champagne and decided that we should christen an old 1957 Oldsmobile I owned. He went out on the street in front of the hotel, toasted Seaman, probably said something about "the river of no return," and then smashed the champagne bottle across the hood of that car.

Maybe it did the car some good. The next week, Jim Roper, myself and two other graduates from PBR School drove it south to attend a Vietnamese language school in Coronado. The car had bad valves and didn't have much power, but somehow it made it over the pass between Bakersfield and L.A. We more or less coasted downhill into the Los Angeles basin and then it was an easy ride to the Coronado Naval Station near San Diego for our last two weeks of training. The time at Coronado went quickly. They couldn't teach you much Vietnamese in two weeks but at least we learned how to say "Go," "Stop," and "Surrender."

The Vietnamese woman who taught the class was very pretty, and we were introduced daily to her *"ao dai,"* the shapely dress put on over pants we would see again in Vietnam. However, I thought then, and still do, that a two-week school in a foreign language was a rather useless exercise. To me, a two-week course in Vietnamese history and culture would have given us better preparation for what was ahead. But it was the Navy way, and so we did it. When the school was over, most of us went home for a two-week leave. After a wonderful vacation over the 4th of July 1969, on the farm where I had been raised in upstate New York, I headed for Vietnam.

PBR ON PATROL, VINH TE CANAL, VIETNAM

Four

Going and Coming

Caskets traveled by jet cargo planes during the Vietnam War, and I never quite decided whether this was a positive or negative development. In previous wars, it could take days for families to learn of their loved ones' fate. Not anymore.

Usually, the only significant delays came when someone was reported as Missing In Action.

Unlike World War II, when whole divisions of men would get on a troop train and be sent to a port of debarkation to get on a ship, people being sent to Vietnam usually went by air. Jet air transport had transformed the country. The logistics of war had changed. It didn't take two weeks to get overseas and land amphibiously on a foreign beach—you could get to Vietnam in a day, and most troops came and went by air. And there would be no more cemeteries left on foreign soil, as was the case in World War I and World War II. Parents and next of kin were notified quickly when a loved one died in Vietnam, and the funeral would follow soon after. There was no waiting for the war to end to have a loved one's remains brought home.

Near the end of my tour in Vietnam, I worked for the Commander of River Patrol Flotilla Five in the Mekong Delta.

One of his jobs, passed on to me, was to answer questions from next of kin or others about the remains of those who had died and were being sent home. I remember clearly the efficiency and accuracy with which U.S. Army Grave Registration handled those requests. In the case of an American killed in action, they knew who he or she was, the date and estimated time of death, the time that the remains had been transported to a central command and, most importantly, when the remains had been transferred to cold storage. (In a tropical climate, it was important to have bodies transferred to a refrigerated morgue facility as soon as possible.) Army Graves, as it was called, could also report when the body had been embalmed, on what airplane it had been shipped and when that plane would land either at Dover, Delaware, on the east coast, or Travis Air Force Base, California, on the west coast. The goal was to have a body returned to the next of kin in seven to ten days.

As we boarded jet airplanes to be transported to Vietnam, most of us thought we would be coming home in one piece, not in a body bag. When you are young, you have a sense of invincibility about your own life. You are bullet proof. Your mind shuts out the possibility that it could be you coming home as a corpse. In early July 1969, I boarded a jet transport at Travis Air Force Base near Sacramento. I remember that my most immediate concern that day was not the possibility of being killed in Vietnam but, rather, about the airplane getting off the ground. As a private pilot in civilian life, I had studied the effects of temperature and headwinds on aircraft taking off or landing, and was well aware that on very hot days it took a lot more runway to get airborne.

I think it was about 102 degrees the day we rolled down the runway at Travis heading for Vietnam. The plane was an extra-long, stretch DC-8, with one aisle and seats on either side. It had a narrow fuselage that seemed as long as a football field with tight seat spacing. The independent contractor who was operating the plane had obviously been told by the U.S. military to fill every seat and to take off with a full load. The plane lumbered down the runway that day and slowly gained speed, though it seemed like it was on the ground forever. Finally, as the white hash marks began to appear marking the opposite end of the runway, the nose of that underpowered DC-8 came up, and we gradually lifted off the hot, concrete runway. For a moment, I thought we might never get to Vietnam.

The trip to Vietnam took nearly a whole day, and we stopped in Hawaii and at Clark Air Force Base in the Philippines for fuel. The demeanor of the men on the airplane was subdued. It was quiet on the plane and not much was said. Virtually everyone except the flight attendants was in a military uniform. Each person, I am sure, was thinking about what was coming next. For all of us, it was a journey into the unknown. Juxtapose that to the spirit of the troops a year later on the day in 1970 when we left Vietnam for the trip home. I will never forget the outburst of relief and joy when the nose of that homeward-bound plane lifted at Ton Son Nhut airport in Saigon headed for the United States. A spontaneous roar went up from the passengers on the flight. It was only surpassed by the near explosion of emotion when the plane landed many hours later in California. I had heard cheers on commercial flights when, after turbulent rides, the pilot would finally get the airplane down at its destination. But those reactions paled with the eruption of emotion from those veterans returning from a war zone. When that flight returning from Vietnam touched down at Travis Air Force Base, a roar went up in that plane packed with men in military uniforms exceeding anything I have ever heard before or since while traveling on an aircraft.

* * *

When we went to Vietnam, there was a common phrase used by Navy personnel arriving called going "in-country". Some of us had been on ships operating in the Western Pacific and, as a part of those deployments, had operated off-shore even, in some cases, entering ports in Vietnam. The one positive aspect of those deployments was that for the time we were in the area we received combat pay of around $100 per month. But, we were under no illusions about the risks being taken. Unless you were a fighter pilot operating from an aircraft carrier, you really didn't see much of the war from a ship. The overpowering presence of the United States Seventh Fleet meant that the enemy, in most cases, confined their combat activities to land-based operations. That also meant, however, that once you were in-country, you were involved in that land war. Although operating on boats on the rivers of Vietnam, we were integrally involved in the struggle to control the land and territory of the country. Being in-country meant being close to combat.

Military personnel bound for the southern reaches of South Vietnam usually flew to Saigon, and, from there, to operating bases throughout that part of the country. Most Navy men were required to report to a military hotel in Saigon for orientation and then reassignment. In its usual, predictable way, the Navy had given a nautical/historical name to this rather moth-eaten place of lodging—it was called The Annapolis Hotel. But that is where any comparison with usual Navy accommodations ended. It was an old walk-up hotel from the French era, four stories high, with peeling paint and without air conditioning. Located in the heart of Cholon, a Chinese enclave of Saigon, the hotel faced a street bustling with commercial and military traffic and was surrounded by the bars and restaurants often frequented by members of the U.S. military. The neighborhood reminded me of the many "sailor towns" that I had seen while on board ship visiting ports throughout the Far East during my first Navy deployment. No visible effort had been made to disguise the Annapolis Hotel. Everyone knew that it was a billeting facility for Navy personnel. It was obviously a place where Americans lived, with a pile of sandbags surrounding the front door and a Marine guarding it with his M-16 rifle. The hotel had no restaurant; we walked down the street to a local café for our meals.

There wasn't much to do at the Annapolis, and so we tended to hang around and await orders to our final destinations. This hotel is also where I had my first introduction to the war. We had returned to the hotel after dinner, and I was sitting in the heat and humidity of my third-floor room cleaning a .45 Colt pistol that had been issued to me that day. A slow-moving ceiling fan was clicking away and I was trying to stay cool by wearing just a pair of shorts. Suddenly, without any notice or warning, there was a tremendous explosion. Dust was everywhere, the ceiling fan broke and fell, almost hitting me, and then I started hearing cries for help down below. I grabbed my .45 and headed down the nearest stair well, not really knowing what I would do if I encountered someone. I had never been in a bomb explosion but no one had to tell me what had happened. The street level entrance of the hotel was demolished and the Marine guard was dead. A Viet Cong guerilla had driven a motorcycle up to the front door, detonated a bomb, killed the Marine guard, and blown out much of the first floor.

Several men who had been watching the evening movie on the second floor were injured. Some BBs and shrapnel from the bomb had penetrated the floor and hit them as they were seated. We later joked about how some of the men would have difficulty trying to explain to their grandchildren that they earned their first Purple Heart in Vietnam by receiving minor wounds in the rump as they watched the evening movie. None of this, though, masked the message that had been delivered by the enemy—this was a wake-up call. This was no longer training camp. This was the real Vietnam and we could expect more of it to come.

*   *   *

Within a week after the explosion at the Annapolis Hotel, my orders came to report as a Patrol Officer with River Division 535 in the Mekong Delta. Most of us were tired and bored, wanted to get out of Saigon and wanted to see where we would be spending our tour in Vietnam. Again, air transportation was the preferred way to travel. River Division 535, at the time, was operating on the Co Chien River, a large branch of the Mekong River. It is located about one hundred miles south of Saigon and snakes its way in a generally west-east direction as it flows toward the South China Sea. Our "mother ship" was a World War II era LST (Landing Ship Tank) that had been outfitted to provide support to PBR's and other Navy boats stationed in the area. Like battleships named for states in the U.S. and cruisers after cities, the Navy often named LST's after counties. This one was called the *USS Garrett County* and had been retrofitted with a large landing deck so that it could be used as a base for helicopters as well as boats in the "Brown Water Navy". It was to that ship that I was transported by an old Korean War vintage Sikorsky helicopter that made the daily mail run to the ship from Saigon. We called it "The Jolly Green". It wasn't an attack helicopter. It lumbered through the air announcing its arrival with a noisy engine and looked more like a moving target than anything else, but it could carry a lot of weight and it was the quickest way to get men back and forth to the LST.

It was there on the *Garrett County* that I would meet Eldon Tozer and my other new colleagues of River Division 535.

The Mekong Delta was then, as it is today, the breadbasket of Vietnam. It was a major source of rice, fruit and vegetable production and nearly all of this produce was transported by boat. Agricultural production and its related commerce in this part of the country were directly related to the mission of the U.S. Navy. The job of the PBR's, in what was called Operation Game Warden, was to stop the trafficking and transporting of arms on the waterways of the region and to open its canals and rivers for the free movement of commerce. It was in implementing this policy that I began my duties as a U.S. Navy Patrol Officer in the Brown Water Navy.

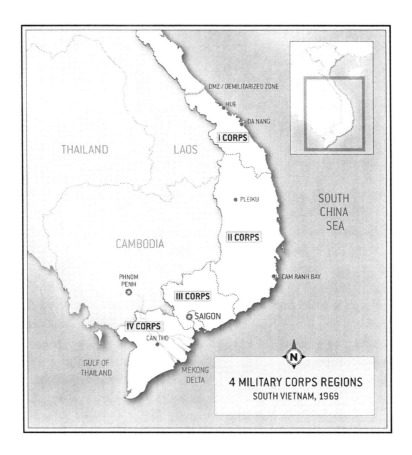

DMZ / DEMILITARIZED ZONE

HUE

DA NANG

I CORPS

THAILAND

LAOS

PLEIKU

SOUTH CHINA SEA

CAMBODIA

II CORPS

PHNOM PENH

CAM RANH BAY

III CORPS

SAIGON

IV CORPS

CAN THO

GULF OF THAILAND

MEKONG DELTA

4 MILITARY CORPS REGIONS
SOUTH VIETNAM, 1969

Five

On Patrol

Just when the river would begin to seem peaceful—and it was beautiful, and outwardly serene—machine gun fire had a nasty way of disabusing us of the notion. I am not sure what prompted me to start writing a journal during my time as a PBR sailor, but it has become invaluable to me. My first entry was dated 17 July 1969.

But first, a word on the assignment that had been given to River Division 535. At the time I arrived, the Division was concentrating its efforts at opening the Mang Thit River/Canal, which connected two major branches of the Mekong Delta to commercial traffic. The Viet Cong were strongly entrenched in the area and had set up toll stations along the canal to tax boats and barges that were using it. As a result of the enemy activity, this primary waterway, which saved dozens of miles in travel for barges and boats on their way to and from Saigon, was essentially closed to commercial traffic. When I flew to the <u>Garrett County</u> on the "Jolly Green", River Division 535 had just started its mission of trying to reopen this waterway. My first entry in the journal read:

> *"Have been in the Division almost a week now. It is just a short time but feel like a veteran already. Have had four indoctrination patrols and*

tomorrow I'm on my own. Here goes . . . hope for the best.

Our mission right now is to try to open and keep open to commercial traffic the Mang Thit Canal that runs between the Co Chien and Bassac Rivers. It is a primary route to Saigon but has been heavily controlled and taxed by the VC. It's about as wide as the Allegheny River in Warren, Pa. but is narrower in spots. Outwardly, it is peaceful and is really quite a scenic river to run. But found out differently two days ago.

Was in a PBR taking a medivac to Vinh Long—a Vietnamese lady injured by a booby trap. All of sudden the radio came alive, someone was yelling and you could hear machine gun fire in the background. You could sense the confusion, fear and initial panic which erupted in the first moments of the ambush. Though I was hearing it only on the radio, I felt as though I were there.

Two B-40 rockets hit the boat. GMG 2 Easton was critically wounded and died later as result of those wounds. An Army Sergeant was also medivaced. Chief Lynch, a member of our PBR class in California, was also on the boat, broke an eardrum and got shrapnel in his leg but he is OK. Was never so glad to see anyone in my life as I was to see him getting off that boat!

It's hard to be analytical about all of this. The bombing of the Annapolis Hotel in Saigon had given me the initial shock to the war so this firefight didn't do that. It did though bring into real focus my own situation. I am going to be on that river

*for the next month or two, and it could happen
to me. Maybe that is what unites all of us here
on the <u>Garrett County</u>—both we and the helo
pilots. It could happen to anyone at anytime—
the eventuality of that is enough to cement any
brotherhood. Whatever else, the war is no longer
a word, a topic for discussion, something that
Bernard Fall or some other author has written
about. Yet, I suppose it is that, but now more than
that. It is a personal conflict of life and death taking
place in a very small world of 50-100 men who
work as a team and as professionals."*

MEKONG DELTA REGION

40

As I reflect on those words, there is a lot which now looks not only like observations on Vietnam but on war and combat generally. The personal camaraderie and importance of mutual support are reminiscent of histories I had read of World War II or even the Civil War. We flew the American flag on our boats, but it wasn't flag-waving that kept you pumped up; it was the realization that you were living in a dangerous and life-threatening environment and that you couldn't exist or survive on your own. In our case, there was also the forced closeness of living for extended periods of time on these small boats which themselves became a part of who you were. To this day, former PBR crewmen hold a love and respect for those 32-foot fighting platforms that we operated in Vietnam. They were small, but we knew and appreciated their strengths: good speed and tremendous firepower. We also knew their weaknesses. They had little protective armament and they couldn't move at all if the jet-water pumps became clogged with weeds. But, while on the river, they were home for us. It is hard to explain, but we became attached not only to our fellow crewmen but to the boats as well. They defined who we were: four or five men on a boat, usually including one or two Vietnamese who were in training, out on our own with only the immediate help of another cover boat for twelve hours at a time on a remote river or canal in unfriendly territory. It all became intertwined like family. And when someone was killed or wounded, it hurt like family.

When you enter the Mang Thit River from the upper Mekong River (Co Chien), there is a small, bay-like entrance to the river with a village at the mouth called Quoi An. The river itself runs for about fifty miles on a meandering north/south heading. Near the southern end, as it enters the lower Mekong River (Bassac) near Tra On, are several miles of straight, man-made canal built, most likely, during the days of French colonization. It was along this extended waterway that we patrolled. In contrast, the main rivers of the Mekong, which we called "the big river", are where our support ships were located. You felt safer on the "big river" because it could be 2-4 miles wide in places. When you think of the large Mekong River, visualize it as you would the wide and expansive sections of the Mississippi River. At times it was so wide that it looked like a large lake, not a river.

In my Journal, I had described the smaller Mang Thit River as about "the size of the Allegheny River, near Warren, Pennsylvania." If you live somewhere else, say in the Washington, D.C. area, you might think of the width of the Potomac River near Georgetown as describing what the wider sections of the Mang Thit looked like. However, on the man-made, canal portions of the river, the channel was much narrower. Here the width of the river was more like twice the width of an average city street. You couldn't turn around in these narrower, canal portions of the waterway without backing the boats down, putting them in reverse and then giving them a hard right or left turn when you started forward again. It was a process akin to what you have to do to parallel park a car or turn it around on a small street. If you were shot at in these areas, there was only one solution—full speed, straight ahead as you tried to get away from trouble.

Though the width of the Mang Thit changed as you moved along it, the water itself stayed the same. The water throughout the Mekong Delta was brown: a dark chocolate brown—the same color as the muddy banks. It didn't matter where you operated, up near the Cambodian border or closer to the South China Sea—the water was always brown. For that reason, all of the U.S. Navy boats that operated here became known as the "Brown Water Navy". Some of the soil and silt in the water had obviously come via the river all the way from China, through Laos and Cambodia and into Vietnam. But some of the color also came from erosion and siltation in the delta itself. The rivers here had strong currents but unlike a normal river, they flowed in two directions, not one. Twice a day when the tide changed, the direction of the current changed, so that at low tide, sand bars and shallow spots could become a problem. Charts and the channels for shipping on the "big river" were generally marked. However, on the smaller rivers and canals like the Mang Thit, navigation was learned mostly on a trial-and-error basis. Most of us had been trained on seagoing ships where radar was a vital tool in navigation. Radar was also helpful on the PBR when you were operating on the main rivers, but we found that it was generally useless as a navigation tool on the smaller waterways. Later, when we got to the Vinh Te Canal on the Cambodian border, we would remove the radar from its mast and replace it with an M-60 machine gun.

Our schedule on the Mang Thit usually consisted of twelve-hour patrols. You either pulled the day patrol—about 6 a.m. to 6 p.m.—or the night patrol, which ran for the other twelve hours. Nearly everyone preferred patrolling in the daytime. The enemy could see you better during the day, but he was also more exposed in daylight. The guerrilla warfare being conducted in this kind of conflict benefited the enemy most at night. Also, you had to stay awake at night—not an easy thing to do at 2 a.m., and sunrise seemed to take forever to happen. Patrols also took on a different character at night. During the day, the river would be full of boats and barges and we would sporadically stop and search vessels checking for contraband. At night, there was a curfew. No civilian boats were allowed on the water. This meant, and our assumption was, that anything moving at night on the river was enemy activity. The civilian populace knew this and kept the curfew. To that extent, there were fewer chances of civilian casualties at night.

Nevertheless, night patrols were more arduous and more tiring than patrolling in the daytime. At night we ran at "darken ship", no lights, and often would float with the tidal currents just waiting and watching for Viet Cong movement on the shore or on the river itself. Most nights were boring and nothing happened, but it was the tension of always being alert during the darkness that made night patrols so hard. During the monsoon season, it seemed to rain almost continually. In Vietnam I learned that a pouring rain at night was a lot more miserable than a hard rain during the day. There is something to the old saying of feeling "wetter than a drowned rat". That was the way you felt coming off a rain-soaked night patrol in the Mekong Delta.

The statistics of the Vietnam War, and probably any war, usually reveal a large number of deaths and casualties due to either accidents or friendly-fire incidents. The second entry in my journal reminded me of one of those events. After the ambush that killed Bobby Easton, the area of that rocket attack was designated a "free-fire zone". On July 18th I led a patrol of 4 PBR's, which I described blandly as "the first patrol on my own and things went pretty well." Yet the rest of what I wrote refreshed my memory of a tragedy that nearly happened.

The ambush that had claimed the life of Gunners Mate Easton came from an uninhabited bank located on a big curve in the river. As the first boat through the free-fire zone that now marked that ambush site, I gave the order to open fire, and we peppered the area with our twin .50's and small arms fire. By prearranged orders, the boats following also opened up with automatic weapons when they got to the same spot. As the last boat in the patrol was coming through, the boat I was on had already gone around the bend in the river. Suddenly I heard bullets swishing past us and realized: "These are our rounds; we have just come around the bend and now are taking our own fire!" I hit the siren, the signal to cease fire, and the firing stopped. According to my diary, this had been a 24-hour patrol. When we got back to the <u>Garrett County</u> I was really tired, which my writing indicates. However, I did write that the incident "created a few tense moments" and "in the process, I goofed when I radioed in my coordinates which put us in a field!" We were lucky that day that no one got hit.

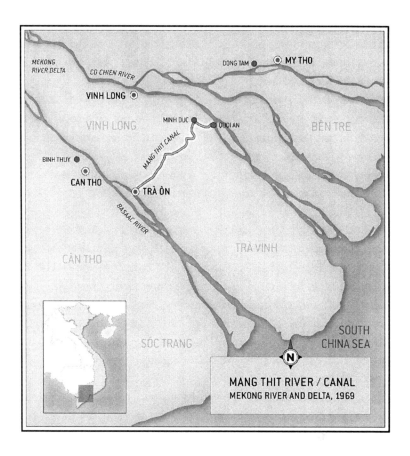

In reflection, this episode reminds one of life in general: you learn by doing and sometimes you are lucky that things don't turn out worse. That particular event instilled in me a newfound respect for the carrying distance of the .50 caliber machine gun, and it was a mistake that I never made again. The truth of the matter is, though, that war is like life; unexpected things happen. There can be unintended consequences; there can be accidents. An enemy bullet can take someone's life but a friendly-fire accident can be just as deadly. Later, in 1970, when I was working on the headquarters' staff for PBR operations in the Mekong Delta, our commander asked me to look into the death of four sailors who had been killed in an artillery attack in an area close to the Gulf of Thailand. What I found out was as tragic, perhaps more so, than a death caused by the enemy. These four sailors were sleeping in a relatively safe base camp when they were killed by an errant shot from a five-inch destroyer gun providing artillery support from the Gulf of Thailand. Either the ship had been given the wrong coordinates or the coordinates were inaccurately entered by the ship's personnel. The result was the same; four Americans were killed by friendly fire. In civilian life accidents can be tragic but, in war, consequences are often multiplied because the tools being used are so lethal.

Prior to entering the Navy, I had studied in a seminary and considered entering the Christian ministry. Needless to say, what I was learning in Vietnam was not taught in seminary. Yet my experience in the military taught me that for most soldiers, sailors and airmen, being a warrior was not a natural American trait. Most of the men I met had also gone to church, Sunday school, or the synagogue. What we were doing now was not instinctual or a part of our upbringing. When tragedy did strike, we went back to our old ways of seeking some kind of solace from our sorrow. I have always had respect for the role of military chaplains. They are a bridge to what we have been and represent hope for what can be. I had not known Bobby Easton. He was killed before I had a chance to meet him. But on July 19, 1969, along with other men from the ship and the River Division, I attended a service led by a military chaplain to honor Bobby's memory. My journal entry of that date accurately reflects what an ex-seminary student probably would have written:

> *"Had services today for Easton. Was a sad moment.*
> *All of the PBR sailors wore black arm bands during*
> *the service. An Episcopalian priest did a fine job.*
> *We affirmed the creed, prayed the Lord's Prayer,*
> *and the priest read some of the great promises*
> *of faith. It was meaningful as something as*

*meaningless can be. Death is a great mystery but
its presence gives a new dimension to life. Life is so
temporary, yet, at the same time, so eternal."*

The men who served on these boats were a microcosm of the
U.S. Navy itself. They had come from aircraft carriers, cruisers,
destroyers and, in my case, mine sweepers. They had been
trained as boatswain's mates, gunner's mates, electricians and
enginemen, but in this new role, as crewmen on a river patrol
operation, they had been transported into a whole new world.
They had to be warriors as well as ambassadors, able to be
tough as well as considerate. They were combatants, but were
being asked to have the discretion of policemen. They had to
be ready to shoot but were also expected to help "win the hearts
and minds" of the local population. I came to have great respect
for these men. Such conflicting demands are not easy to juggle.
They worked hard at a very difficult job.

From time to time, during daylight hours, we would be asked to
take food and rice to remote villages along the river as a gesture
of good will, as a part of what was called the "pacification"
program. In one case, sailors from our River Division helped
some Army advisors pave a muddy village plaza with fresh new
concrete. On another occasion, they helped build desks out of
leftover ammo crates for a local school. Instead of dumping cans
of food they didn't like from the C-rations we were issued, they
would toss them to villagers along the way. Admittedly, they
did not have the sophistication and training of Peace Corps
volunteers, but they were good humanitarians. What can you say
about men who do that and then, when the sun goes down, don
flack jackets and helmets and drift on darkened boats waiting for
an attack? If nothing else, they were resilient. At their best, they
were good ambassadors for their country under very challenging
conditions.

There was another facet in living with these men that I also admired—their sense of humor and their ability to make light of their own situation. Some deep thinkers in Saigon had come up with what was called "psy-ops", psychological operations. The general gist of this type of warfare was to try to strike fear into the hearts of the enemy. In most cases, what it meant for us was to put loudspeakers with a big amplifier on our boats and then cruise down the river at darken ship (no lights) with a Vietnamese message blaring away into the darkness about why the enemy should come over to our side. Most of the men thought it was a joke. After all would you be moved to change sides in a war if you were on the receiving end of such a message? There was one tape, in particular, which the men called the "spook tape". It sounded eerie and sort of weird, like ghosts speaking to each other. The gist of it, we were told, was that a Viet Cong guerrilla had died and had gone to hell instead of heaven, and that because of being on the wrong side, he was now in deep agony. If only he had come over to our side, things would have been a lot better and now, instead of being in hell, he would be in heaven! The intent, supposedly, was to entice enemy soldiers to get so angry that they would open fire on us, divulge their position, and then we could call in artillery or air strikes on them. Most of our sailors (and I must include myself in that) thought that it was all a bunch of hoo-ha that somebody up the chain-of-command had cooked up, and who probably, himself, needed psychological help. But, again, the Navy wanted to do it, so we did it. It always engendered a lot of laughs from the troops.

It was also interesting how connected we were to what was going on in the United States. We never lost touch with the music or news from home. Listening to Armed Forces Radio was like listening to your local DJ at home, and we always had AM/FM radios on our boats to pick up the news. The Robin Williams depiction of being a disk jockey in the movie "Good Morning Vietnam" was right on, as far as I am concerned. One announcer, who came on the radio early in the morning, often ran a spoof detective piece called "Chicken Man". The PBR sailors thought it was a hoot to listen to, especially if they had survived the night without a firefight. One morning, as the boats were coming in from a night patrol, the Chicken Man radio vignette was being broadcast. At the end of each of each of these episodes, the radio announcer would yell: "Chicken Man, Chicken Man. He's everywhere! He's everywhere!" Just as that happened on that particular morning, one of the PBR boat captains keyed the microphone on the official, covered, encrypted boat radio that was used for command and control throughout the Mekong Delta. I am sure that every boat crew in the Brown Water Navy was laughing when "Chicken Man is everywhere!" went flooding across the official airwaves. Obviously, it didn't go over very well with the brass. They were soon firing back on the radio: "Knock it off! Security on the net!" Yet those were occasions that you always remembered as moments when the real world from back home provided a welcome relief from the daily grind as we knew it. Americans, even in tough situations, were looking for a reason to laugh.

Sometimes the news from home would run into events not as pleasant. My journal entry of July 25, 1969 reads:

> *"Today, Captain Walt Gutowski with the MATS team at Minh Duc was wounded while on a sweep with the VN's (Vietnamese troops). Hit a booby-trapped 105 mm. Howitzer shell. Looks like he'll make it without losing a leg. Had Major Willoughby on the PBR when we got the word. Went up a small canal "on step" (high speed) to get there. Got there just as the helo did, and we were able to help him get out on a stretcher and over to the helo for medivac . . . I knew him fairly well . . . He was conscious, tried to be cheery, and was saying: "I'm going to make it. Charlie didn't get me yet, etc."*

On the same day, according to what I wrote, Armed Forces radio and the *Stars and Stripes* newspaper were reporting that: *"Senator Edward Kennedy today said he was considering resigning from the Senate because of the controversy over the drowning incident of a girl riding in his car."* In Vietnam we were never very far from the news. The news on Walt Gutowski also turned out bad. I noted in an entry dated August 8 that he had died from his wounds.

Perhaps the most poignant description of working in a combat zone while still staying connected to America back home took place on July 21, 1969. There was some contact that day with the enemy:

> *"Today, confiscated a sampan. Man beached and ran. VC had an ambush set up for us on the southern part of the Mang Thit. We mortared the area and then went through at flank speed with guns blazing. No trouble. Think he (VC) lost interest. Tonight our boats set an ambush in the area where our man (Easton) was killed. VC in sampan opened fire. Sea Wolves (Navy helicopter gunships) and artillery called in. No friendly casualties."*

However, the journal also noted that: *"The cosmic news of the day, of course, was the moon landing. An incredible feat and definitely marks the dawning of a new age."* How we witnessed the moon landing was incredible in its own right. When we would leave our LST "mother ship", which was anchored in large Co Chien branch of the Mekong River, we would travel downriver to where the Mang Thit River/Canal began. Just inside that river entrance was the small village of Quoi An. Attached to the village was a barracks building surrounded by barbed wire which housed four or five U.S. Army advisors. When the PBRs began patrolling the Mang Thit, we made regular stops at locations like this to check in with the Army and to pick up any intelligence that we could. To say the least, these soldiers welcomed our presence because we also provided them support and a way of escape in the event they were attacked. In Quoi An, these Army advisors had run a power cord from their portable generator to the local village marketplace and installed a television set in the small gazebo that was the village center. It was the only television in the village and seemed to be of immense interest to the village residents.

On July 21, 1969, we made our usual stop at Quoi An and found a hubbub of sorts in the marketplace where the TV set was located. Everyone was talking and pointing at the television. I asked the Vietnamese officer whom we were training what it was all about. He said: "Americans are landing on the moon, but the people here don't believe it. They think that it is some kind of American trick just being done on television!" Of course, our boat crews were also interested in seeing it, so everyone went over to watch the moon landing. Here we were, in a remote village in Vietnam watching Americans landing on the moon with people who didn't believe it was happening. It was one of the incongruities of the war which I have always remembered. Disney or Hollywood couldn't have invented something like this, but it was reality on the Mang Thit River in 1969. There was always something new or unexpected that could happen when you were on patrol in the Brown Water Navy.

QUOI AN MARKET PLACE, 1969

OLD DESTROYED FRENCH CHURCH ON THE MANG THIT, 1969

Six

The Vietnamese

August 25, 1969 was the first day I wrote about a new Vietnamese officer I was training, Thu Trung Van. At war, you meet many people. It is impossible to know that moment of meeting that your life is about to change forever.

After a few days on patrol, Thu and I became close friends. I knew that I could trust him, that he was a fighter, that he made good decisions, that he was a good human being, and that he spoke excellent English and would talk openly and candidly about his country and the war. I have always had an inquisitive streak and, on that particular day, Thu accompanied me on a visit to a Cao Dai temple, which was visible from the river. The Cao Dai was a religious sect that I had read about before going to Vietnam and, at least early in the war, had been opposed to a communist takeover in the south. My observation is undoubtedly based upon what Thu had taught me that day:

> *"Visited a Cao Dai Pagoda down near the Mang Thit bridge with Lt. Thu. A very interesting religion which uses the lunar calendar. The "temple" almost looked like an astrologer's laboratory. Their central symbol is a big eye painted on a blue sphere symbolizing the universe. It is*

supposed to represent, I guess, the all-seeing eye of God. The swastika is also used—an ancient Vietnamese symbol for peace."

I learned a lot from Thu over the course of the two months we spent with each other in boat training. He became, for me, the course in the culture and history of Vietnam that I had wanted back at language school in Coronado. He was one of four children and his father had worked for the national railroad under the French colonial government. Because of his father's job, Thu had traveled around the country. For a time, he also lived in Cambodia while his father worked there when that country was a part of French Indo-China. When the French lost their war to Ho Chi Minh and the Viet Minh in 1954, Thu's family moved back to Vietnam. Under the Geneva Convention ending the war, Cambodia and Laos became independent countries. His father had to choose where he wanted to be a citizen and decided to return to his ethnic roots in Vietnam.

Thu was college-educated, having graduated from the Vietnamese Naval Academy at Nha Trang, the South Vietnamese equivalent of the United States Naval Academy at Annapolis. Like all young men in South Vietnam, he was subject to being drafted into the Army. He decided, instead, to join the South Vietnamese Navy. Thu was knowledgeable about his country, and he respected and understood its culture. He was also anti-communist in his sentiments. He did not see a future for his country under a communist dictatorship. He also liked Americans and was ready to learn what we could teach him about the PBR, its capabilities and how we were using it to patrol the waters of the Mekong Delta. I immediately felt fortunate to have met Thu. His language skills helped me to better understand the country and to communicate with those we met on our patrol duties. After he left our River Division, he became Executive Officer in one of the South Vietnamese units that were taking over the Mekong Delta patrol boat effort as America exited the war.

Our friendship remained intact during the rest of my tour, and we stayed in touch. Before I left Vietnam, Thu had moved to a Vietnamese Naval Base at My Tho. One day while on Navy business in My Tho, I contacted him. He invited me to go to Saigon and have dinner with his family—which was a real treat. There is nothing as pleasant as a sit-down meal with a Vietnamese family. Americans, with our fast food habits, don't understand how to sit down, relax, drink, eat and just enjoy a long three or four-hour-long communal meal. It's the kind of event that enables you to see inside another culture. It was probably there, the afternoon and evening of that extended family dinner, that Thu and I became friends for life. I will never forget the ride we took to get to that dinner. We drove from My Tho to Saigon with me on the back of Thu's 75 cc. Honda motorbike. Route #1 in those days was a two-lane, pot-hole-filled highway jammed with jeeps, trucks, buses, old cars and military vehicles of all types. We zipped along in and out of traffic and, at one point, witnessed a helicopter air strike off to the west. It was a country at war and at commerce all at the same time. It was a country I came to like and understand better thanks to my friendship with Thu Trung Van. When he calls me today, he still stays "Hello, Trung Uy"—the Vietnamese translation for Lieutenant JG.

WITH THU ON PBR PATROL ON THE MEKONG RIVER

*   *   *

It has been roughly forty years now since the end of the Vietnam War and most Americans have lost touch with this time in our history. Why were we there? What were we trying to save or protect? What made Vietnam important?

The answers are complex, not easy. In many ways it was a war that America wandered into. Before volunteering to go to Vietnam, I had read many books and articles dealing with these questions. Probably the most helpful were the books written by Bernard Fall. Fall had a very interesting background: a Frenchman born in Austria, a teenage fighter in the French underground during World War II, a political science professor at Howard University in Washington, D.C., an author and historian, and an on-the-ground war correspondent. By chance he decided to write his doctoral dissertation at the Johns

Hopkins University School of Advanced International Studies in Washington on the subject of the Viet Minh who, at that time, were at war with the French in Vietnam. With his own money, in 1953, he financed a trip to Vietnam to view first-hand the fighting that was going on. Thereafter, he became entranced with what was happening in this Southeast Asian country and wrote seven books about what he witnessed there. Perhaps his most famous book for American readers was *Street Without Joy (1961)*, which dealt with the fighting, over many years, in Quang Tri Province. It would be there, in Quang Tri, on an operation with the U.S. Marines on February 21, 1967, that Bernard Fall would be killed, the victim of a Viet Cong booby trap.

I have always had great respect for wartime correspondents and writers who travel to the areas where the fighting is going on. That, in my mind, sets them apart from the armchair journalists, who sit back at headquarters or somewhere behind the frontlines and pontificate and hypothesize about what is happening at the front. Edward R. Murrow and Ernie Pyle were frontline reporters in World War II. David Halberstam was like that in Vietnam, as were Peter Arnett and an old friend from the Associated Press, Jay Sharbutt.

I met Jay Sharbutt and Horst Faas, a Pulitzer award-winning photographer, in 1969, when they covered the operation we were engaged in along the Cambodian border. In 1970, when I was working more directly in the "Vietnamization" campaign of the U.S. Navy, I periodically traveled to Saigon. I would stop to see Jay at the AP offices and, on a couple of occasions, he invited me to the official 5 p.m. briefing held by the U.S. military on what was happening in the war around the country. Jay referred to this daily routine as "the five o'clock follies." It usually started with a reciting of the official body count of enemy killed in South Vietnam during the prior 24-hour period. Jay Sharbutt and many of his colleagues knew that the real story of what was happening in the war could not be found in that room. Jay had learned that first-hand by being one of the only reporters on the ground during the earliest days in the vicious fight at "Hamburger Hill." Yet, when I met members of the press in Saigon, it amazed me how many of them wrote stories based only on what they heard at that daily press briefing. Their bylines would say "reporting from Saigon" implying to readers that they had actually been out with the troops, but many of them never left the armchairs of their air-conditioned offices in Saigon. It could be dangerous to leave the relative safety of that city to go to places where the war was actually being fought.

Bernard Fall was respected by men like Jay Sharbutt because he hadn't stayed at headquarters in a cushy office. Fall's trip to Vietnam in 1953 had been to the countryside north and west of Hanoi where the war was being waged. He not only wanted to know what the French fighting forces were doing; he wanted to understand what was motivating their enemy and how that fit into the long-term history of Vietnam. He was passionate and uncompromising about what he wrote. In a book of previously unpublished writings assembled by his wife after his death, *Last Reflections on a War, (New York:Doubleday, 1967)* Dorothy Fall relates the antipathy her husband met from the French when he began reporting the truth about the success of Ho Chi Minh and the Viet Minh in North Vietnam. In 1957, three years after the Viet Minh victory at Dien Bien Phu, Bernard Fall went back to Vietnam, this time to the South. The 1954 defeat of the French in the French Indo-China War led to the creation of two Vietnams: North Vietnam, controlled by Ho Chi Minh leading a communist government; and South Vietnam, a non-communist government, more supportive of the French and with a growing relationship with the United States.

Bernard Fall was a journalist with a critical eye. He was not an automatic "yes man" for the South Vietnamese regime. In 1957, when he went to the South, he began publishing stories of the weaknesses and corruption in the Diem government that was running South Vietnam. He was no lover of the communists, but he also knew that a corrupt government in the South was no solution to the problems of Vietnam. His observations were met with criticism by many of the hawks in the United States who were advocating greater military intervention in the country. Again, according to Mrs. Fall, his observations, like those he had made in 1953, were not welcome in some quarters. "Several job offers were rescinded, but he held his ground. He was aware of memos circulating and of false accusations, but he would not compromise." (Ibid., p. 10)

For readers today, Bernard Fall's critique on what was happening in Vietnam more than fifty years ago may seem unimportant or irrelevant. However, it reflects an attitude we often see in policy makers even today. There is a tendency to equate patriotism with military intervention and to question critical thinking as somehow un-American. The truth of the matter is that, in the 1950s and early '60s, had we read the history of Vietnam more thoroughly and made decisions based more upon actual fact than what we wanted to hear, our country and the world would have been much better off. Though President Kennedy had authorized ramping up military advisors in the early 1960s, he still had questions about how far America should go in trying to fix a problem in Southeast Asia that had essentially been left in our laps by the French. Even President Johnson expressed concern about sending troops to the mainland of Asia, but he finally succumbed to the worry about America appearing weak and irresolute. Bernard Fall's death in 1967 stilled one of the voices of caution about the limits of what could be accomplished militarily in Vietnam. Just one year after he died, in 1968, after the political success of the Viet Cong and North Vietnamese in their Tet Offensive—American public opinion began to change significantly. To the surprise of most Americans, largely due to growing opposition to the Vietnam War, Lyndon Johnson announced that year that he would not seek re-election to the Presidency.

I gained a new appreciation of the long-term history of what had been going on in Vietnam as a result of reading Bernard Fall. At one time, before the French colonized the area, Vietnam had been self-governing. Though plagued by political rivalries, the Vietnamese had, by the beginning of the nineteenth century, established a distinct and independent nation. Throughout their history, they maintained a dislike and hostility toward the Chinese who for many years had occupied parts of Vietnam. There had also been periods of conflict between Vietnam and Cambodia along Vietnam's western border. The Vietnamese were proud of their history of independence, which was interrupted by the arrival of the French in 1856. France ended Vietnamese self-rule and replaced it with a colonial administration that included all of Indo-China.

The history of the twentieth century in Vietnam became characterized by a rising hostility to the French and a drive by the Vietnamese to regain their independence. Vietnamese students, who went to Europe and France for higher education, picked up western ideas of liberation and self-determination. One of these students, Ho Chi Minh, became the standard bearer for the reunification of the country. He helped create the Viet Minh to fight against the French, led these forces during World War II to fight the Japanese occupation, and then, after the war, took up arms again against the French. At the end of World War II, his pleas to the United States and the West to recognize Vietnamese independence fell on deaf ears. The world was essentially silent when France reoccupied its Indo-China colonies at war's end.

Could it have been otherwise? The well-known American diplomat, George Kennan, testified before Congress that it could have ended differently. Kennan had been Ambassador to the Soviet Union during its formative years and knew first-hand of the aggressive intentions of Stalin and international communism. He believed that as the United States had helped contain Russian aggression in Europe by recognizing the independent state of Yugoslavia under the leadership of Marshall Tito, so Ho Chi Minh could have served a similar purpose in Southeast Asia. In 1965, appearing before the House Committee on Foreign Affairs, Kennan argued that communism was not as monolithic as many experts were alleging, that there was a great deal of tension between Russia and China, and that a huge American military build-up in Vietnam might actually mute those differences and result in the two major Communist powers becoming more involved in that part of the world. In his report to the committee he wrote:

> *"I would be the last to generalize about such situations, or to suggest that a hands-off policy is everywhere possible and desirable. But there is one thing we might usefully bear in mind. The surest way to invite a strong and effective Communist involvement in situations of this nature is to involve ourselves heavily, particularly in a military way . . . .*
>
> *The less we are in the picture, the less is there any excuse for actual military intervention on the part of the Communist powers and the greater are the chances for rivalry between Moscow and Peiping for political dominance in the region concerned . . . Where this Chinese-Soviet rivalry exists, the local regimes, whether nominally communist or otherwise, are almost bound to begin to act independently in many ways—to develop, in other words, Titoist tendencies."* Bernard Fall and Martin Raskin, *The Vietnam Reader*, (New York:Vintage Books, 1965), p.16.

Unfortunately, Kennan's views also fell on deaf ears. He had been marginalized as a retired Ambassador who was out-of-touch with the American mainstream. (It was Kennan, back in the early days of the Soviet Union, who had warned of what he saw coming as Russia began to flex its muscle and begin its own dark descent into Stalin's dictatorship.) His cautionary views on U.S. intervention in Southeast Asia became a minority view as President Johnson ramped up the war. By the end of 1966, there were over 350,000 American troops in Vietnam. Before the war ended that number would climb to half a million.

The impetus for the war on the American side was driven by an ideological rationale called "the domino theory." The concern was that if Vietnam fell to the Communists, then the rest of Southeast Asia would soon follow. It was easily believable. The cold war started with the expansion of the Soviet Union into eastern Europe, and the United States was instrumental in the creation of NATO and other alliances in western Europe to stop it. President Truman called it a policy of "containment" to help stop Soviet aggression. The mistake made in Southeast Asia was to assume that all of these same dynamics were at work in Vietnam. As Bernard Fall and George Kennan were observing, tremendous fissures had developed between Russia and China. Vietnam and China also had a long history of hostility toward each other. In 1978, three years after the end of the Vietnam War, Vietnam and China reverted again to their historic differences and fighting began again along their common border.

Interestingly, during World War II, Americans had worked behind the lines with Ho Chi Minh in fighting the Japanese. In addition, President Roosevelt had voiced to the British and the French that Americans were not fighting World War II so that these European allies could retain their colonial empires. At the Tehran Conference in 1943, FDR had actually advocated that a trusteeship be established to take control of French Indo-China once the war was over, and remarked that "after one hundred years of French rule the inhabitants were worse off than they had been before." (Fall, *Last Reflections on a War,* op.cit., p.128.)

However, President Roosevelt never got a chance to implement his vision for Vietnam—he died in 1945 just months before World War II ended.

Ho Chi Minh and his Viet Minh forces were briefly in control of the country at the end of the Second World War, but French forces soon returned to Vietnam. Ho's guerilla fighters then retreated to the mountains north and west of Hanoi and continued their fight for independence. That is where Bernard Fall found them in 1953. It was not until 1954, after their devastating defeat of the French at Dien Bien Phu, that the Vietnamese would regain control of the country. The Geneva Accords that ended the war with the French made provision for the establishment of separate countries in the north and south. As a part of that agreement, a vote on unification was to be held in 1956. However, fearing that Ho Chi Minh would win the election, the South Vietnamese government squelched the referendum. It was never held.

By 1956, both the Korean War and the cold war had significantly changed the thinking of policy makers in Washington. Now, the focus would be on battling communist expansion no matter where it occurred. There was little consideration in co-opting a nationalist movement, though it was communist, as had been done in Yugoslavia. Instead, steadily, slowly, surely, Americans began to replace the French in Indo-China. The first name on the Vietnam Wall in Washington, D.C. is of an American killed on June 8, 1956, but the actual beginning of significant involvement by the United States started even before the French pulled out in 1954. Unless somebody stopped it, we were sliding into a war. It would be a war against communist expansion. It would also be a civil war and revolutionary war for unification and independence.

Aside from understanding the history of Vietnam and what got us there, Bernard Fall also correctly predicted what it would take to win the war. He had a formula that he touted: RW = G + P—revolutionary warfare equals guerilla warfare plus political action. We Americans were good at the warfare part of this formula. What we couldn't do was the "political action" piece. This had to be done by the South Vietnamese. No foreign power can prop up an unpopular regime or create an effective government in someone else's country; this can be done only by those indigenous to the land. It was Fall's view that of the two aspects of revolutionary warfare, the political action or governance issue takes primacy.

> *"The 'kill' aspect, the military aspect, definitely always remained the minor aspect. The political, administrative, ideological aspect is the primary aspect. Everybody, of course, by definition, will seek a military solution to the insurgency problem, whereas, by its very nature, the insurgency problem is military only in a secondary sense, and politically, ideologically, and administratively in a primary sense. Once we understand this, we will understand more of what is actually going on in Viet-Nam . . . ."* (Ibid. p. 210)

This was written before I went to Vietnam, but I found it to be true once I got there. We were winning militarily and had crippled the North Vietnamese and Viet Cong in their 1968 Tet Offensive. But the political issue, the trust of the people in their own government, was not strong in the South and there was very little that Americans could do about that. Some believed that we could have won the Vietnam war by unleashing unlimited warfare upon the North, but that wouldn't have resolved the problem of governance in the South. In 1956, Ngo Dinh Diem, the South Vietnamese President, had made the foolish decision of abolishing local and village government. Instead, he appointed military district chiefs to run government at the local level. Local, village self-government had historically been a bedrock principle of governance under old Vietnamese regimes and even under the French, but now it was abolished. Diem was assassinated in 1963, but the aftermath in Saigon was more political instability with a succession of military coups taking place and a continuing, rampant system of governmental corruption. Since the beginning of our involvement, Americans never had a strong partner on the political side in South Vietnam. All of the military might in the world wasn't going to win this war.

The United States had also invested millions of dollars in "pacification" programs aimed at strengthening the South Vietnamese presence in the countryside, and U.S. Navy boats in the Mekong Delta were a part of that. We periodically stopped at villages to hand out rice, soap and Vietnamese flags. On one occasion, on the Mang Thit River, we joined with the Army in paving a marketplace in Quoi An Village. We also worked with a local Catholic priest in building desks for a school, which we made from leftover ammunition crates. The State Department and American military throughout the country made noble efforts to address the poverty and educational needs in the country, but it was like swimming upstream. It was hard to make progress when the government in Saigon was so swamped with corruption and bureaucracy.

In 1969, on a patrol on the Vinh Te Canal along the Cambodian border, a Vietnamese officer and counterpart whom we were training came to me and spoke about a problem at a local outpost. The soldiers at this outpost were outraged because they were getting paid twice but could only keep the money from one paycheck . . . the second payment was "going to the generals in Saigon". I sought out the American colonel who was the chief advisor in the area and he told me: "Yes, it is true, it is an outrage, but there is nothing I can do about it. It is a way of life over here." The more I thought about it, the more angry I became. Here we were, risking our necks everyday trying to help this country, and American aid was essentially paying for the war. Now, I had proof that the military establishment that ran the South Vietnamese government was not only running an illegal pay-off scheme but it was ripping off the American taxpayer! Sometimes discretion is the better part of valor, but this time I decided to jump the chain of command and I wrote to a Congressman (Lee Hamilton) whom I had met in Indiana. To his credit, he had the matter investigated and confirmed. But nothing happened except the U.S. Army Colonel got reassigned. The double-pay scheme continued. It is hard to win a war and win the heart and minds of the people when this kind of thing is going on.

*   *   *

Whatever your views may be on the North Vietnamese leader, Ho Chi Minh, there seems to be common agreement on two matters: (1) He was a forceful leader with a driving purpose. His goal was to rid Vietnam of all foreign powers and to unify the country. In that sense, he became the "George Washington" of Vietnam. (2) He led by example. He was the leader of a poor country and as so disdained the accoutrements of power. He wore peasant clothing, led a somewhat reclusive life, never married and became known to his people as "Uncle Ho". Today, when you go to Hanoi, you can visit a Russian-style mausoleum and look at his body. But the more powerful symbol of the grip he had on his country is the nearby bungalow that he lived in during the war years. This small, nondescript house is nearly within eyesight of a large, ornate, former Governor's Mansion that had been built by the French. Yet Ho Chi Minh rejected that mansion and made this bungalow his state residence. He was asking the people of Vietnam for incredible sacrifice, and he would live simply and Spartan-like in a small house . . . the only tip to modernity being an underground bomb shelter to escape American air attacks.

More that forty years after I met Thu Trung Van, we would have the chance to remember our time as Naval officers during the Vietnam War. We would experience again the culture of this country, and compare it to what it had been, what it has become today and where it is going. We would retrace our journey as young men. And he would offer me a simple piece of advice.

"You can joke about anything in this country," he would tell me, "including the corruptness and incompetence of the government. But you can never criticize Ho Chi Minh. He is revered in the South as well as the North as the man who unified the country."

As Moses never saw the "promised land", so "Uncle Ho" would not live to see a united country. He died in 1969, and the war went on without him. But the armed forces that he had led and helped create would finally succeed and would overrun South Vietnam in 1975. That would also change the life of Thu Trung Van and of thousands of other Vietnamese who had supported the South. Under the threat of spending years in detention camps and prisons, they would have just hours to make life-changing decisions: remain in their homeland, or flee their country and seek a new life in other lands.

PHOTO OF HO CHI MINH'S BUNGALOW IN HANOI

Seven

Happenings

In our operations on the Mang Thit River/Canal, we worked with U.S. Army personnel. The Military Advisory Command Vietnam (MACV) was organized into teams that were assigned to various provinces in the country. In our case, we were working with MACV Team 68 which was headquartered in the city of Vinh Long. From Vinh Long, these advisors were sent to district towns like Minh Duc, where Walt Gutowski, whom we had medivaced, was assigned. The village of Quoi An, where we witnessed the landing on the moon, was similarly home to three or four U.S. Army advisors.

Those of us on PBR's sometimes felt isolated and exposed when we operated in two-boat patrols miles from our home base. However, compared to these Army advisors, I felt relatively safe. These poor guys were living right in the middle of Viet Cong country, and their only real defense came from some poorly-trained militia units who lived in the small towns. Some of the Army men were there because of their careers. They had chosen the Army and the Army had put them there. Others, like me, were reserve officers who had been subject to the draft and were serving shorter terms of military service. One of these Army reserve officers, stationed at Quoi An, was probably serving at the most isolated of all assignments, the MAT level, Mobile Advisory Team. I described him this way:

> *16 August 1969: "Have met another real character in the Army—1st Lieutenant Guy Powers with the Quoi An MAT team: a complete Ivy League intellectual, a grad student at Columbia University majoring in Romance languages. He conversed today with the priest in French. He is a complete cynic about the war, always arguing with his senior officer, an ex-enlisted man. I enjoy pushing his buttons to get him going on politics, the war, etc. He was nearly killed when the 9th Infantry platoon he was leading was overrun near Dong Tam. He says that they had contact with the VC everyday. Apparently, the VC concentrated in that area in an attempt to kill as many Americans as possible. This has kept pressure off areas like Vinh Long where there are no regular U.S. units fighting."*

What Lt. Powers was putting his finger on was the relative perception of risk. He actually felt safer in a small compound of three or four Americans in Quoi An, surrounded by hundreds of people who couldn't speak his language, than he did in a large American outfit like the 9th Infantry Division. He felt less targeted in such a small, isolated place. It seemed rather odd to me at the time, but if your platoon had been overrun by the enemy, maybe it was a good assessment. Guy Powers couldn't wait to get out of Vietnam, and he didn't like the Army. I will say this for him though. When it came to civic action work like building desks for a school or paving the courtyard of a community marketplace, he was right in it, leading the show. The Catholic priest we met had helped us organize a joint Army/Navy effort to build desks from old ammo crates for a grammar school located near Quoi An. Powers was an example of the equalizing or leveling factor we knew in Vietnam because of the draft. Without a universal draft, you would not have found many graduate students in Romantic languages in the Army. Because of it, people like Guy Powers were there fighting along with everyone else.

WITH GUY POWERS AND A CATHOLIC PRIEST FROM AP PHOUC ORGANIZING A PROJECT TO BUILD DESKS FROM AMMO CRATES FOR A LOCAL SCHOOL LOCATED ALONG MANG THIT RIVER.

* * *

We would cut the tassel on our berets only after our first firefight. When my time came, I found that my training took over.

The word "firefight" was commonly used in Vietnam. In the Navy it meant that you had exchanged fire with the enemy. I recorded what I called my "first firefight" on 28 August 1969:

> *"Had my first firefight this morning at an island on the Co Chien River. It was brief but real. We were drifting with the ebb tide. SM1 Jarvinen was in boat #729 and SM1 Williams was in boat #863. #729 drifted into the beach and stayed there. We (#863) stayed out in the river and kept close by using our engines. At about 0315, the boat on the shore opened fire with an M-60 machine gun and an M-16. They saw a man crawling up toward the boat in the grass. There was a brief cease fire and one of the Vietnamese crewmen yelled at them (the VC) and told them to surrender. Then there was a loud blast of a grenade going off and #729 opened fire again.*
>
> *We popped a flare, #729 pulled off the beach and reported two wounded. We rendezvoused and I judged the injuries to be minor shrapnel wounds. We then both made firing runs on the beach— negative return fire. Transferred the wounded to my boat, and we headed to the* USS Jennings County. *Jarvinen stayed on station. Chief Lynch and his patrol went down to the area, put in more fire and then searched the area. I came back with more flares and we continued the search. Saw two enemy during the engagement and believe we killed them both, but the search produced negative results. Blew up one sampan believe belonging to the enemy.*

It was a relatively minor engagement but it is good to get the first one over with. At least, I know that I can react with a certain amount of logic and good sense. There was no confusion between units during the action. Cut the tassel on my beret [inaugural right of first firefight], and now feel something of a veteran. Wounded men, Goodall (U.S.) and Trang (VN) are in the Binh Thuy hospital and okay. They are expected back in about a week."

This incident reflects one fact about combat as I experienced it in Vietnam. It happened very quickly and was over quickly. We described our patrols as "weeks of boredom and moments of terror." The momentary nature of these encounters was due, in part, to the fact that we had tremendous firepower that we could bring to bear on the enemy, especially from the air. A corollary to this was that on the Mang Thit River we were generally fighting a guerilla force with limited manpower. Their advantage was darkness and surprise. They would hit and run. It was not to their advantage to stand, fight and slug it out.

*　*　*

The incongruity of the Vietnam War could mean going on an airstrike, then going to church.

The use of airpower in Vietnam requires an understanding of the role played by the helicopter. Unlike World War II where there were no helicopters, or the Korean War where they were primarily used for medical evacuations (medivac), in Vietnam they became the workhorses of the war in terms of transporting men and arms as well as in aerial combat support. We got to know the highly-trained and skilled Navy helicopter pilots because they lived with us on our mobile support bases. This was especially true on the LST "mother ships," where a flight deck had been installed for landing and supplying helicopters. The call sign for these choppers was "Sea Wolf", and they were always a welcome sight to PBR sailors operating on the rivers and canals of the Mekong Delta.

On two or three occasions, I went on helicopter missions. A part of my motivation was that I had learned how to fly a plane in high school and, as a result, had a great love of aviation. I also found that viewing our area of operations from the air was helpful intelligence since most of the time I was seeing everything at ground level from a boat. Though I loved to fly, in many ways I did not relish the responsibility imposed on these helo pilots. They controlled tremendous firepower, which also meant destructive power. They were operating in an arena in which it could be difficult to distinguish friend from foe. My journal describes both the thrill and the peril of aerial warfare:

> *"22 July 1969: "Went on a helo strike and "reconned" the Mang Thit. Great fun riding in those birds. Tremendous amount of ammo wasted on the strike. Although air power and the helo have been a key factor in this war, I still doubt its effectiveness as a discriminating weapon. Awfully easy to shoot innocent people when you are seeing them from 500 feet."*

Five days later, I went on another helo strike. It was a Sunday, and I wasn't scheduled for a patrol. I got back to the ship in time for Church.

> *"Sunday, day off. Went up on a helo strike again and took some photos. Exciting to ride on low level runs. However, became more leery of some helo targets. Saw men running toward an area of supposed VC activity. Shot at them and they were probably killed. Received no fire back. Pilots were*

convinced they were VC, but how can you be sure at 500-1000 feet? Back at ship, worship led by Episcopal priest, Chaplain Westling. Creed and prayers again . . . there is a real sense of history in that Church."

It is bizarre now to read a journal entry like this combining going to church with an air strike, but Vietnam was that way. You lived in at least three worlds: the old ship Navy, the new river boat Navy, and the old ways of back home. It was all jumbled together and was kind of mind-boggling. I was learning a lot of lessons, including the fact that technology and air superiority had limitations and were not enough, on their own, to win a war. There was also the realization that, in general, there were usually fewer civilian casualties when you were fighting on the ground, yet even with the best efforts, civilians could still get caught in a cross fire.

26 August 1969: "Today was another day of picking up the pieces. Medivaced 4 VN civilians—3 women and a little girl. All had been wounded in an Army sweep in Xua Hiep and most probably by helos. One was very pregnant. The other got a 7.62 round through both legs below the knee and severed an artery. We took her to the Mang Thit bridge and the U.S. Army got a medivac chopper (Dustoff) in. Shows again the tragedy of war—they (Vietnamese soldiers) killed 4 VC today but look at the innocent who were wounded. We went down a small canal to get them [the wounded civilians] as a part of the operation. It was so small and narrow that we couldn't turn around and was lined with heavy underbrush. Talk about feeling vulnerable!"

*   *   *

By early September, our River Division had been transferred to a land base at Binh Thuy, which also was the headquarters for PBR operations in the Mekong Delta. We began to patrol the Mang Thit River/Canal from its southern terminus on the Bassac River near Tra On. That meant that we had a long ride on the "big river" (in this case the Bassac) in transiting to and from our patrol area. It was also an area where we had very few navigational aids and our charts were inaccurate. I still have memories of making this long run from Binh Thuy down to the Mang Thit. The river was very wide so you felt very secure. It made it difficult for the enemy to shoot at us, especially when we were running at full speed. Coming off patrol on the narrow Mang Thit canal, you appreciated the wideness of the big river and knew that in an hour or so you would be back to the comforts of the base at Binh Thuy. Upon reaching the big river, you could take off your helmet and flack jacket, lean back with the wind in your face, let your body relax and look forward to getting home.

One night, after we had been relieved from patrol duties, we were in this laid-back mode on the big river with both our boat and our cover boat flying along. It was a beautiful night, the stars were out, and we had left our patrol concerns behind. We were thinking of getting back to the barracks for some much-needed sleep. Suddenly the boat slowed down then stopped dead in the water. We looked over the gunwales and found we were on dry land! We had gone aground on an uncharted sand bar. It was quite a scene. Men got out of the boats and tried to push and pull them to no avail. With no alternative, we decided to wait for the tide to come in, then slowly wiggled the PBRs back out into deeper water. We were so far from shore that not even the VC could have seen us, although they may have heard us swearing and yelling as we tried to extricate ourselves from the sandbar. Finally, as the sun was coming up, we were fully floating on the incoming tide and, with some chagrin, continued our trip back to home base.

When we operated from a land base like Binh Thuy, we were subject to military rules on liberty, including a curfew. Military personnel were required to be back at their base around sunset. Because it was air-conditioned, we would hang out at the officer's club and listen to the scuttlebutt of what was going on with other outfits in the area. My Journal entry on September 16th reflected the news of the day and none of it dealt with our River Division:

> *"Sunday night three big incidents: (1) A LTJG was drunk and driving a jeep after curfew. It overturned. He was banged up and a LCDR with him broke an arm. (2) A guy from RIVDIV 572 went berserk at the EM [Enlisted Man's] Club. They took him to the 29th Evacuation Hospital, and he ended up cutting a bunch of wires in the generator room so that they lost power. (3) An Army guy went berserk on liberty. They had to strait-jacket him down. In taking him back to his unit in a helo, he got loose and jumped out of the bird. He was killed, of course. You hear of such incidents but they usually don't happen altogether like this."*

Two days earlier on my 29th birthday, 14 September 1969, I had written a rather terse and somber entry:

> *"'I am poured out like water and all my bones are out of joint; my heart is like wax.' (Psalm 22) Today is my 29th birthday. I wrote a 'once-in-a-lifetime' letter. It could turn out to have serious repercussions, but I was compelled in good conscience to take the step. Not to, would have meant the unnecessary loss of life in the war. It was*

*a small effort and probably won't succeed, but at
least it was something."*

What prompted this entry were discussions I was having
with some patrol officers from another River Division. They
had received orders to go to a place in South Vietnam where,
historically, the Viet Cong had always been in control—the U
Minh Forest. It was quite possible they were being sent to their
deaths. During all of the long years of the war, nobody had been
able to make any significant inroads into this overwhelmingly
enemy jungle stronghold, and it held no strategic value at this
time in the war. I was outraged by the decision, though it didn't
directly affect me.

We had been taught in Officer Candidate School to obey orders
coming down the chain-of-command. However, many of us
were reserve officers, civilians with a limited time commitment
to active duty in the Navy. I found that reserve officers were
more circumspect about blindly following orders. Most of us had
no plans of making the Navy a career. If we received orders, we
obeyed them, but we also discussed the wisdom, justification and
reasons for an order. I had and still have great respect for the role
of reserve officers in the military; they bring common sense and
reflection to the process of military decision-making.

By late 1969, official U.S. Navy policy was in full gear to turn patrol
boat operations over to the Vietnamese. Why now send American
boat crews to an area of Vietnam which the South Vietnamese
themselves had written off? Why get involved in a whole new
field of operations whose only success would be tallied in body
counts? The more I spoke with fellow patrol officers about this, the
angrier I became. Some "deep thinker" or "genius" at the upper
echelons of the Navy in Saigon must have concocted this idea as a
way to make a late impact in the war—but to what end? We were
"Vietnamizing" the war; it was not a mission that would have an
effect on the outcome of the war. The only certainty was that more

Americans would be uselessly killed. It was a situation in which I may have been naïve, but I decided to write a letter to Congressman Lee Hamilton about it. My journal entry expresses a concern that there could be "serious repercussions" from doing it. Jumping the chain-of-command was a no-no. I didn't know what would happen if the Navy found out, but it wouldn't be good. In the end, there was no reprimand or repercussion. I remember being concerned enough with what I had done to tell a fellow officer, Larry Forbes, about it. Most likely, my letter was futile and resulted in nothing. But my recollection is that the U Minh operation was never fully implemented, so maybe it did some good.

* * *

Another entry from September describes the brutal realities of the war. War is a nasty business and the enemy was good at it. Periodically, the reality of being a combatant on the receiving end of the way they made war would hit home.

> *"Last night at Minh Duc we found a body floating in the river, hands tied behind the back and bullet-riddled. Looked like a VC execution. Badly decomposed with bad odor. PF's [Provincial Forces, low level and often undependable] would have nothing to do with it. I guess the VN's really have a phobia about bodies. My crew was also reluctant to get involved—mainly because of the smell. I tried to drag it with a boat hook but was unsuccessful, so notified the U.S. Army at Minh Duc and they investigated. Definitely, one of the more "gory" episodes I have witnessed."*

It was a lesson in warfare that I was beginning to learn— brutality is effective. The enemy was good at it, better than we were, and didn't like it when the tables were turned.

Eight

Warrior

If you ever met Capt. Bob Olson, you would never forget him. He was a statement. The first time I saw him, he was sitting on the edge of an old French gunboat drinking a beer with an AK-47 in his lap. He wore Vietnamese black pajamas, had no helmet and was enjoying the afternoon. I am sure he saw me as a "green-horn," which I was, with a .45 strapped to my waist, wearing a helmet, dressed in fatigue greens and wearing a flack jacket. But he was immediately friendly. He said, "Hello, how're you doing?" like we had been long lost buddies. We took to each other. He did not lack confidence, and I wanted to learn. It was a good combination.

I had heard about Olson from other U.S. Army soldiers stationed along the Mang Thit River in their MAT Teams or District towns. They were all a part of the same Army Advisory Team #68 headquartered in Vinh Long. Most of them worked in small teams but they had told me that Bob Olson would be working by himself with the Vietnamese. According to Mike Paluda, who had preceded Bob Olson in the same position, Olson was advising the Vinh Long Battalion, a Vietnamese infantry outfit that had been around since the French days. Though land-based and Army, this battalion also had access to some old French gunboats that they used in the waters throughout Vinh Long

Province. Unlike the Regional or Provincial Militias, which consisted of part-time soldiers whom we derogatorily called the "Ruff-Puffs," the soldiers of the Vinh Long Battalion were full-time and well trained. As Paluda described it, "These troops went to work in the Army every day, but essentially lived at home when they were not out on operations." He also observed, "Bob was a great soldier; he loved those troops, and they him. He was very enthusiastic about doing his job with these Vietnamese soldiers."

As we talked by the side of his boat that day, Olson told me that he was on his second tour of Vietnam, that he had lost a lot of friends in the country on both tours and that his *modus operandi* was to take the fight to the enemy. From what I could tell he spoke relatively good Vietnamese, and he used the language to get close to the troops he was training. He thought the black pajamas, the uniform of the peasant farmer and the enemy, sent the right message. The AK-47, used by the enemy, was also his weapon of choice; he thought it more reliable and effective that his own M-16. Soon after our introduction, he started to talk about doing some joint operations with the PBR's and quizzed me about my schedule and how we could link up and do things together. After a few minutes of conversation, I realized that I had met a true warrior, a professional who knew his trade, and who was fearless in the mission he was executing. He was not a West Point or ROTC product. He had been drafted, came up through the ranks as an enlisted man, and was selected for and graduated from Officer Candidate School. The Army was his life.

Maybe he was testing me for reliability, but the first operation I worked on with him was a solo mission. We picked him up one night on a PBR and moved upriver under cover of darkness. There was an old French church on the Mang Thit that had been destroyed in some previous fighting, and we had been told not to go ashore there, that the area was booby-trapped. Olson showed no concern about that. We got to the Church around 10 p.m. and he said, "Put me ashore. Pick me up at 3 a.m. Give me two flashes of your flashlight before you come in. I will return it with four flashes for proper identification. If you don't get four flashes, don't come in." We left him, backed off the beach, used our engines sparingly and stayed in the general area in case he needed help. We heard no gunfire during the night. At 3 a.m., we slowly approached the old Church. A hundred yards or so from shore I signaled with two flashes from the flashlight. Four flashes came back in return. We eased in to the beach, and he jumped aboard in his black pajamas.

As we backed out and got into midstream, I asked him what had happened.

"Got one!" he said.

"But we heard no gunfire. How did you kill him?" I asked.

"I didn't want to make a lot of noise," he responded. "A Viet Cong came over to where I was, squatted down in the darkness, and addressed me as 'Comrade.' I had a pop flare in my hand, so I turned it sideways and zapped him with it."

I had never before heard of using a pop flare as a weapon. It was a hand-held flare, which went up when you hit the bottom of it to provide nighttime illumination. That night, Bob Olson had sent a message that there was a new and determined fighter on the Mang Thit River. You didn't know where he would show up, and anything lethal would be used as a weapon. A pop flare could go up in the sky. It could also penetrate a human body.

A week or so later, we were on a day patrol. Captain Olson preferred working at night because that was when the enemy was most active. However, on this particular day, he had scheduled a sweep along the river through a small village where he thought we might find some enemy contraband. We operated from the PBR's and inserted him and a few Vietnamese soldiers at the edge of the village. I asked him if I could go along, and he agreed. (I'm not so sure that my own commanders would have said, "okay" had they known I was going on a sweep with Bob Olson, but they were back on the *Windham County*. I was in charge of this particular patrol.) So I stepped off the boat with him and his troops carrying my own M-16. We started moving from house to house through the small community strung along this part of the river. Most of the houses had walls of thatch and a roof made from palm fronds. They were commonly called "hootches" by Americans.

We came to a more permanent building with walls of stucco. Olson described it as a "Buddhist temple," and we approached it warily. He went in and I followed. It was one large room with an altar or shrine at one end. Suddenly, there was a flurry of noise at the opposite end of the room. Without saying anything to me, he swung his AK-47 toward that end of the room and opened fire. He hit a rooster that was banging its wings and trying to get outside. I yelled, "Jesus Christ, Bob! Take it easy, it could have been a kid." He calmly looked at me and said, "Don't preach to me. On my first tour over here, I went out with a whole platoon and was the only one to walk back. I shoot first and ask questions later." I never "preached" to him after that. He was operating in a world that I didn't fully understand.

On another night mission in the middle of a monsoon rain, I picked him up again by boat. This time he was with only two or three men from the Vinh Long Battalion. The weather was so bad that I was amazed we were even going out. Olson viewed bad weather as a positive factor. It was a good night for his kind of operations. "They won't be expecting anything," he said. His plan was to set up an ambush site on a trail that came down to the river's edge in an area that we knew was used by the enemy.

When we got to where the trail met the river, he showed me where to meet him and his men, again scheduled for about 3 a.m. Then he told me the rest of the plan. "Don't drop us here. Take us about a kilometer downstream. They will be expecting us to come in here where the trail meets the river." So we went downstream with the PBR and landed him and his men on the same side of the river about a mile from the trail. "We are going to walk back through the rice paddies for about a kilometer, and then we will come back to the trail. They won't be expecting that. Pick us up at the usual time with the same flash light signals." With that admonition, with the rain pouring down, with a poncho as protection from the weather, some explosives and his AK-47 in hand, he and his Vietnamese soldiers stepped off the boat.

A few hours later at the appointed time, we approached the rendezvous point. I signaled with the flashlight and he responded. We picked him up, soaked through to the skin, along with his men. This time he said nothing and I didn't ask him what had happened. Instead, he picked up the microphone of an Army radio and called Army headquarters. "Vinh Long," he shouted, "this is the big ranger! Three Victor Charlie [Viet Cong], Kilo India Alpha [killed in action]. Out!"

Then he turned to me and said, "We'll get three more in the morning."

"How is that?" I asked.

"We strung a trip wire and killed them with claymores [mines]," he explained. "Then we put three grenades under their bodies and pulled the pins. We'll get more in the morning when they come to get the bodies."

The effect of Bob Olson's work on this river was dramatic. I made a note in my journal that after about three weeks of his exploits using these tactics, hostile action on the river had dramatically decreased. War is a brutal business. Captain Bob Olson understood that. He could dish it out just as brutally as the enemy, and they didn't like it. Attacks against the PBR's began to diminish. Within two months, his work, combined with our continuous patrols, had changed life on the river. Commercial boat traffic was again moving along the Mang Thit, much of it headed for Saigon, and the Viet Cong stopped taxing those using the waterway. Bob Olson taught me a lot about the realities of war. I largely credit him with making our lives safer on that river. I could never have done what he did. Sometimes I didn't agree with the way he operated, but what he accomplished was inarguable. Normal reasoning and accepted conduct, as I knew it, didn't necessarily work on the battlefield. He also taught me a new appreciation for the combat infantryman. I had always believed that being on the ground, in the infantry, was what really made the difference in war. Now that I had experienced it, at the tutored hand of Bob Olson, I knew that it was true.

In looking back, I believe that what impressed me most about Olson was his professionalism. He knew that he couldn't win the war by himself. He also realized that America could not win this war without the support of the Vietnamese. Therefore, he dedicated himself to teaching these Vietnamese soldiers the skills of a warrior as he knew them. Bob Olson was a complex and smart man. We talked about policy, about the military strategy in Vietnam, and about what was going on at home in the political arena. He had his views and I had mine, but our discussions were invariably civil and enlightening. I always looked forward to seeing and talking with him when I would start out on a patrol. I knew that when I stopped at wherever his outfit had beached their boats, I was going to hear some interesting commentary. He was also probably going to talk with me about an operation he was contemplating, a new approach at hitting the enemy. He was never static or predictable in what he was about to do. He knew that doing the unexpected would throw the enemy off balance, and that keeping the Viet Cong second-guessing was a good military tactic.

Because of his skills as a warrior and because of the risks he took, many of us didn't expect him to outlive the war. We thought that in one of these middle-of-the-night encounters, he would get unlucky and be killed. What we weren't ready for was his death by accident, by an ambiguity of war which was not related to being hit by a bullet or being at the wrong end of a grenade attack. My journal entry of 8 August 1969 on the occasion of his death succinctly summed up what happened to him:

> *"Had a depressing experience yesterday. Captain Robert Olson (USA) was killed in a drowning accident. He was on the way to a night ambush on the Mang Thit in a Boston Whaler. The VN's with him panicked and the whaler overturned. Everyone made it out but Olson. It was so unreal for him to die that way. All of the danger he had been through and then this.*
>
> *Olson reminded me of Lawrence of Arabia, such an utter professional and yet so complex. The night before we had a long conversation, and I felt like I was getting to know him . . . . Such absurd events really sober you up and completely dash away any war concepts of gallantry and honor. So far, over here, I have been picking up the pieces."*

The night that Bob Olson was killed, I was patrolling with the PBR's upriver, about two miles away. We received a radio report that there had been an accident, and so we sped down to the area where he had been working. As I recall, the old French gunboats operated by the Vinh Long Battalion were still pulling men out of the water. Soon all hands were accounted for except for Captain Olson. It was evident what had happened. He had been operating a small Boston Whaler which probably should have had only four or five men in it. Since more men had volunteered for the operation, he had put about ten men on board. It was dark and he was headed out to an ambush position on the river. The big old gunboats were providing cover, following him from behind. The whaler was overloaded and began to take on water. People panicked, and the boat started to swamp. Everyone ended up in the water.

We looked for him all night to no avail. The Army ordered in an old C-47 aircraft which we called "Puff the Magic Dragon." It was often outfitted with machine guns but that night it was dropping flares. They were incredibly bright and illuminated the river, almost like daylight, but our search was unsuccessful. We ended our patrol without finding him.

The next day, while on patrol, we received a radio message that his body had been found in a fisherman's net. We took our boats to help retrieve it. When I saw Bob Olson, it was evident that he had been swimming when he was killed. His shoes were off, he was shirtless and he had shed the bandoliers of ammunition that he often carried. There was a gash in the back of his head. It looked like he had been hit by the steel bow of one of the old gunboats or perhaps had been hit by a propeller. He was a good swimmer and was extricating himself from the accident of the swamped boat. However, it was dark. The heavy gunboats couldn't see in the darkness and their noisy engines would have masked the yells of anyone calling out.

He died a soldier but not as he probably thought he would, escaping from a swamped boat on a river in the brown waters of the Mekong Delta.

Four days later, I took a boat up the river to Vinh Long where I joined Bob's Army colleagues for a memorial service for him and for Lt. Walt Gutowski, another member of Advisory Team #68 who had been killed. Mike Paluda, who attended that service, wrote to Bob Olson's nephew: "Perhaps his enthusiasm and aggressiveness is what led to his death . . . Bob was a great soldier who loved his job and his soldiers. And he was my friend. May he rest in peace."

I am fortunate that I could also call Bob Olson my friend. His name is engraved on Panel 20W, Line 109, at the Vietnam Wall. He is buried in his hometown of Britt, Iowa.

* * *

It is easy to say that you want to "pay your respects" to someone, but what does it really mean? It has always been my view that funerals and memorial services are meant as much for the grieving as for those being grieved. I felt that way on August 12, 1969, as I took a boat up to Bob Olson's memorial service in Vinh Long. I really hadn't known him that long—only about a month—but I felt a part of his family. Maybe it was the intensity of the relationship, serving with him in combat. Maybe it was the recognition of what he had taught me about risk and war. But, ultimately, I think, it came down to friendship. You didn't have to know people very long in Vietnam to get attached to them, and when they were Americans, they were automatically teammates, pals or buddies. You had to count on each other in conducting these operations. I had never felt as American as I did in Vietnam. We were all in the soup together. When someone you knew died, it was like a brother getting killed. It hit you deeply. Your motivations for being there were really irrelevant. You were there and so was everyone else, for one reason: to carry out the policy of your country in a nation at war. It glued you together whether you liked it or not.

I sensed that I was still paying my respects when, in December 2011, I walked into Lois Olson's home in Phoenix, Arizona.

She is a native Iowan, but now lives with Don, a companion of fifteen years. Lois explained that they would be married, but with Bob's Army pension, she is better off staying single. Don also came from Britt, Iowa, but, like Lois, retired in Arizona. Lois and Bob's daughter, Pam, lives nearby and is another reason why Lois now calls Phoenix "home." Bob Olson had told me that he was married and had a young daughter whom he had barely met—she was only a year old when he was killed. Lois speaks fondly of their daughter and her accomplishments: "I am the only one she has, and she is the only one I have; she wanted me to be closer to her."

Then Lois turned to Don who was in the kitchen and asked, "Don, don't you think Bob would have been proud of her?" Don replied, "Absolutely. She has done great!"

Lois and Don go north in the summer, where they usually stay at a cottage Don owns in Minnesota. However, they spend most of the year in Arizona. They are very happy together. The morning we met, they welcomed me with coffee and some delicious sticky-bun rolls that Don had made. After some brief introductions, we started to talk about Bob Olson.

Bob grew up on a farm, an only child. He and Lois had met at a roller skating rink. "When I first met him, I just couldn't stand him!" she said with a laugh. "He was a show-off on skates. At first I didn't like him, but then I guess I loved him enough to marry him."

Lois was three years older than Bob and had graduated from high school in 1951. "Bob should have graduated in 1954," Lois told me, "but he never graduated. He got mad at a shop teacher and quit—I'm not sure if it was his junior or senior year. It wasn't until he was in the Army that he got his GED." When she told me that, it reinforced my impressions of Bob as being a determined and focused individual. With no high school degree, he had set out to become an officer in the U.S. Army, and he had accomplished it.

"We both liked to roller skate, and after we got married, we ran a roller rink," she continued. "But then, in 1958, he was drafted. At the time, he was also helping his Dad on the farm. Probably, because he was an only child, he could have received an exemption from the draft board to work on the farm, but he didn't." Lois also related that Bob had talked her brother, Gordon, into joining the Army at the same time, and they both were sent to Fort Hood, Texas. "I think Gordon thought that he would probably be drafted, so he enlisted to be in the same place as Bob." But Lois recalled that the attitude toward the military with these two friends was entirely different. "My brother hated every minute of it," she explained, "but Bob loved it! My brother got KP [Kitchen Patrol] almost every weekend, but Bob never got it. My brother even blamed the Army when his dog died."

Lois moved to Fort Hood with her husband and, when he was sent to Germany, she went with him. After the tour in Germany, Bob indicated that he wanted to stay in the Army, but Lois wanted to go home, so Bob left the Army. They went back to Britt, Iowa, but Bob wasn't happy. "He got out for a year," she said, "but he was always talking with the Army recruiter in Britt. He came home one day after one of his chats with the recruiter and said that he wanted to go back in the Army. 'Well,' I said, 'if that is what you want for your career, you should go back. If I decide not to go, I'll stay here.' But, of course, I stayed with him."

After he rejoined the Army, Bob Olson was sent to Korea for a year. While there, he was selected for Officer Candidate School at Fort Benning, Georgia. After Fort Benning, Lois accompanied him to new postings at Fort Carson, Colorado, and Fort Leonard Wood in Kansas.

When Bob was killed in Vietnam, she was living with Pam back in Britt, Iowa.

"To me, Bob was very smart and a strong leader," I said to Lois. "He also seemed to like the Army a lot."

"He loved it! He loved it! He loved it!" she immediately replied, "and he was a good leader. One of his uncles said that if Bob had survived the war, he would have become President of the United States. "Isn't that true, Don?" "That's right," Don replied. "He was smart, likable and maybe he would have become President."

"What makes me so sad," Lois continued, "is that just before he died, he wrote and told me that in 22 days he would be going to an office job and wouldn't be going out on any more missions. Before he died, Pam and I went to Hawaii and met him for R&R. She was a year old then. She was so cute, so cute! He would be pretty proud of her today. She is a nice girl and has done well."

In outlining his Army career, Lois described her husband as a gung-ho soldier. "He always wanted to be an officer and, when he went to Fort Benning, he got everything he could: ranger training, parachute qualification, and survival school. Everything they offered. Also, while he was there, I was voted the lead officer wife for the auxiliary. So that was nice."

After Fort Benning, Bob Olson received orders to Fort Carson, Colorado. "He had a wonderful Colonel there," Lois said, "by the name of Ted Swett. He died just last year, but he and Bob were very tight. After Bob died, he would invite me to reunions but I never went. I told him that if I were to go, I would be crying all the time, so I didn't go. 'Maybe it would be closure for you. We would all have open arms for you,' Colonel Swett said. Maybe it would have been that way, but I was still bitter; I am still bitter. I can't help it but I am."

At that point, Lois choked up. "I know that Bob loved the Army. That's what he enjoyed. He told me once, 'If I die with my boots on, I die happy.' I always remember that. But one reason I'm bitter is because Pam never had a dad. All she knew about him was from a picture; she called it 'Bobby-Dad'. That's one reason I'm bitter, and the other is that Bob was afraid of nothing. Because of that, he would volunteer for anything, and I don't think he should have. But that's a part of him I couldn't change."

Tragically, that was the part of Bob Olson I knew best. Lois was right. He was fearless.

Mike Paluda wrote that perhaps Bob's "enthusiasm and aggressiveness" had contributed to his death. That was undoubtedly the case the night that he invited too many Vietnamese soldiers to accompany him on the small boat he was taking out for an ambush. To me, that decision had seemed an avoidable mistake. The boat was just too small for so many men. Yet it might be better to characterize it the way that Lois Olson saw him: he was fearless and, because of that, he volunteered for anything, including jamming as many men as he could onto a very small boat for an ambush operation on the Mang Thit River. Fear is something that he instilled in the hearts of his enemy. If he experienced it himself, he never showed it.

As I have reflected on what Lois Olson told me, it reveals what I believe is a common issue for the families of those who serve in the military. There is a knowledge or experience gap between what is going on at home, and what is happening in combat. It is such a big gap that it really can't be talked out. The world between the soldier and his family proffers silence, not understanding. There is no way that Bob Olson could have explained to his wife what he was doing, even had he tried. The tragedy of a death in war is that it freezes that silence. It is a part of the collateral damage that happens when a loved one doesn't come home. I empathize with the agony of Lois Olson and what she has gone through since her husband's death. I'm just not sure that there is anything that could have been done to change it.

Getting to know Lois Olson was gratifying, though I know that it wasn't easy for her reliving those times long past. We finished our conversation with some discussion on how she was told of his death, what the funeral was like, and some of the issues that she had to deal with after it was all over, including taking care of the farm that had been left to him in Iowa. She also had to learn about what her rights were as a surviving Army spouse. For several years, the Army sent her a pension check, but she found out that it was being paid based on a Sergeant's salary, not that of an officer. Thanks to the networking available through the Gold Star Wives, who meet for the purpose of helping each other with mutual problems, the matter was rectified. "When it was corrected," she explained, "I received a check for past compensation, and it came at a good time. It enabled me to buy our daughter a car for college, and for me to get a second-hand car."

As our conversation wound down and it was getting time for me to go, she again mentioned her daughter. "Speaking of Pam," she said, "she had to work and couldn't be here today, but she wanted to be sure I had my picture taken with you. Can we have one taken outside in the sunshine?" So we walked out on the patio where the beautiful morning sun was warming the air after what had been a rather chilly start to the day. Lois was still healing from a knee-replacement operation, so we sat on lawn chairs in their charming front yard amid the desert and the cactus which, in Arizona, is their lawn. I must admit that I was a little drained, and I am sure that she was, too. I had made a new friend, but it came at the cost of remembering things that sometimes are not easy to discuss. It was clear to me, however, that after all these years, she was still in love with Bob Olson, and that if this day were the same day that he had told her he wanted to rejoin the Army, she would again give him the green light to do so, just as she had back in 1962. And she wouldn't stay home, just as she hadn't when he rejoined the Army back then. She would again support him and accompany him in a career in the U.S. Army, wherever it would take them.

ARMY CAPTAIN, ROBERT OLSON

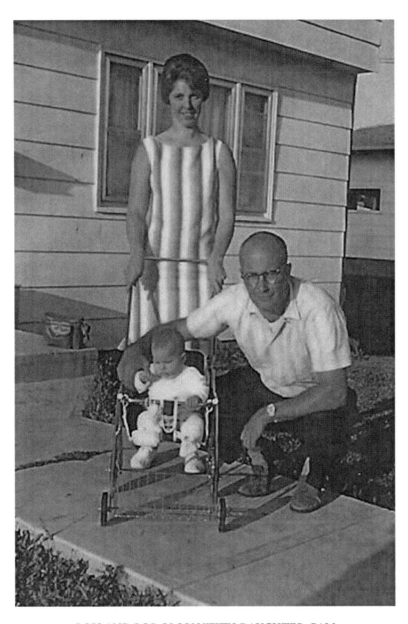

LOIS AND BOB OLSON WITH DAUGHTER, PAM

BOB OLSON TRAINING VIETNAMESE SOLDIERS

BOB OLSON ON PATROL, READING A MAP

Nine

Border Interdiction

My Journal entry of 24 September 1969 belies the fact that all hell was about to break loose:

> *"Well, we've started patrolling the Vinh Te Canal at Chau Doc. It promises to be a rather tedious task—there has been no action for two months. The canal is about as wide as an average street in the U.S. and runs straight as an arrow, paralleling the border with Cambodia. There are four Boat Divisions on about 40 kilometers of canal, so it is quite crowded with PBR's. Actually, the terrain is beautiful—miles of flat, grassy, rice fields flooded by the monsoon rains. Several mountains, VC controlled, jut up from the plain, the most conspicuous being the 'Seven Mountains'. The people along the canal seem friendly, and it appears that VC and NVA infiltration is non-existent or, at least, at a very low rate . . . ."*

The part of this analysis about the natural beauty of the area was right on target. It was, and still is, one of the most spectacular landscapes in Vietnam. It could be a painting on a living-room wall: rice fields, blue sky, and brown water all framed by mountains in the distance—a portrait of the gnawing beauty of the Far East. However, my initial impression of the military situation along the Vinh Te Canal was totally wrong. There hadn't been a lot of fighting here yet, because there had been no one there to contest control of the border. Once we began our boat patrols with the express purpose of slowing or eliminating enemy crossings back and forth between Cambodia and Vietnam, the action would explode.

*   *   *

When you look a map of Vietnam, you are immediately taken by the long, narrow, linear configuration of the country. From its northern border with China to its southern tip on the Gulf of Thailand is a distance, as the crow flies, of over 1000 miles. That is about the same distance as flying from New York City to Miami. Multiply this distance by the additional miles of bays, inlets and rivers that run along the eastern side of the country and by the twists and turns along its western edge, and you have more than 3000 miles of border. That the United States or any country could ever conceive of controlling this kind of real estate and eliminating unauthorized border crossings is hard to comprehend. That, in the end, we would fail in this mission, and that the enemy would use this advantage in geography to move men and supplies into Vietnam to finally win the war, would have been a more realistic military assessment.

In studying war and in the reading of history, the first thing I do is go to a map. Most human conflict has been fought in places with significant strategic or tactical issues related to geography. Americans trying to secure the borders of Vietnam was akin to the British trying to secure the borders of the thirteen colonies during the Revolutionary War. The British controlled the sea and enforced a very efficient embargo along our eastern shore until it was ultimately broken by the French Navy. However, the British were no match for the Americans on the land. The British could not control the interior borders of a country which ran for more than 1000 miles through the hollows and back country of Appalachia from New England all the way to Florida. The North Vietnamese and their Viet Cong allies in the South similarly controlled the western borders of their country. They had built an intricate system of roads and trails to move soldiers and supplies through the mountains along the boundary with Laos and Cambodia. Americans called it the "Ho Chi Minh Trail," and the enemy was in control of most of this terrain. The southernmost 80 miles of that border ran from the City of Chau Doc on the Mekong River to the Village of Ha Tien on the Gulf of Thailand. It was called the Vinh Te Canal, and had been built by the Vietnamese in the 19th century to delineate the border between themselves and their long-time enemy, Cambodia. It is where I found myself in September 1969 when the U.S. Navy started to restrict the movement of the enemy along this border. It wasn't to be the cake walk I had originally predicted. The Viet Cong and North Vietnamese fought back with a vengeance.

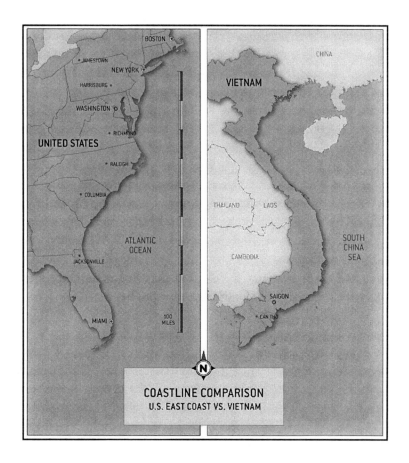

**A COMPARATIVE VIEW OF THE EAST COAST
OF THE U.S. AND VIETNAM**

The operation along the Vinh Te Canal was part of a larger effort that the Navy called "Sea Lords." Navy forces would be used throughout the Cambodian border area of the Mekong Delta to carry out border interdiction. It was here that I would be introduced to what PBR sailors called "the heavies." We also called them "RAG boats" because they were a part of the River Assault Group activities throughout the Delta. RAG boats, unlike PBRs, were not made of fiberglass. They were made of steel, and most of them were also protected by bar armor consisting of welded rebar (like the kind used in construction) affixed to their gunwales and vertical surfaces. In some cases, between the bar armor and the steel skin of the boats, Styrofoam was installed to help quell the effect of shrapnel. The enemy's choice of weapon against the RAG boats, as against the PBRs, was the B-40 rocket. It could be held and shot by one man and, on impact, would spread deadly shrapnel over a large area. The RAG boats had been designed so that a rocket would explode on impact with the bar armor. That would dissipate some of the energy of the weapon; the shrapnel would be captured or diffused by the Styrofoam, and the steel hull would help protect the crew. Because of their armored hulls, RAG boats were designed to slug it out with the enemy. They did not have the speed and elusiveness of the PBR, but they had as much or more firepower, and they could survive ambushes better.

Though I questioned some of the tactical decisions made by the Navy in Vietnam, like placing fiber glass patrol boats whose defense was speed and maneuverability (PBRs) into static, defensive, ambush positions, I was always impressed with the ingenuity which had created the river craft employed in the war. The RAG boats were a good example. The Navy had taken LCMs (Landing Craft Mechanized), who most in the Navy called "Mike boats," and adapted them for the kind of warfare going on in the Mekong Delta. The LCM was originally designed as an amphibious landing craft to take men and material ashore in World War II. In Vietnam, these vessels continued that role but were re-engineered to provide additional combat support functions. The Tango boat (Transport) could carry troops for insertion but also had a flat steel cap over the cargo bay which could be used as a helicopter landing pad. The Command boat had been reconfigured to accommodate an air-conditioned radio room and control center. The Monitor was an LCM in which the cargo bay had been eliminated in favor of a flat steel surface on which was mounted a 105-millimeter

Howitzer artillery piece. It resembled the first ironclad ships used by the Union during the Civil War which were called by same name. Perhaps the most unique boat in the RAG forces arsenal was the Zippo. It had the configuration of a Monitor but, instead of a Howitzer, was armed with a flamethrower that was very effective at dislodging enemy troops who hid behind the dikes and berms of a canal for their defense. It was probably the most feared weapon employed by the heavies. When you saw it in action, you knew you didn't want to be on the wrong end of it.

There were other technical innovations to which I was introduced on the Vinh Te Canal. The United States had provided us with the best tools available. In addition to helicopter support, we were supported by a twin-engine, propeller-driven attack fighter/bomber called the OV-10 Bronco. The plane carried five-inch Zuni rockets, which had incredible destructive impact. Carrying a two-man crew, they often operated at treetop level; you could hear them coming before you saw them. The sound of these aircraft caused fear and dread. Their Navy call sign was "Black Pony." You felt safer when they were in the area.

Perhaps the most interesting technology we had were new, electronic devices. To help us spot the enemy on the move at night, we used "starlight" telescopes, which helped illuminate the darkness with the ambient light from the sky. The landscape presented itself in various shades of a chartreuse green. It was hard on the eyes, and we rotated the use of the scope between crewmen every few minutes. Somehow, despite the use of this equipment, the enemy still found ways to set up ambush positions. The starlight telescopes were good, but so was human ingenuity. It takes more than technology to win a war.

While operating along the Cambodian border, we were also introduced to a seismic listening device. It was well suited to our situation, since there were various trails or paths that came from

Cambodia (only a mile away in most places) directly toward the Vinh Te Canal. We often set up positions at or near these trails. The Navy deep-thinkers in Saigon had euphemistically named these locations WBGP's, military lingo for Waterborne Guard Posts. In effect, they were ambush locations. We were to ambush the enemy before they could ambush us. Since we couldn't see everything with the starlight telescope, at dusk, while we still had visible light, we would set these sensors out along the trails leading to Cambodia. During the night, the crew would take turns on the boat wearing a set of headphones, listening for movement along the trail. Sometimes, if the B-52's were dropping bombs in the area, it felt like we were in an earthquake, and the sensors would go crazy with beeping and background noise. However, they were essentially designed to track the linear movement of troops coming down a trail, so we usually put the number one sensor out furthest from our position, then number two, etc. In total there were about four of these sensors.

Once, at about 2 a.m. with the sensors set, I started to hear beeping on the headset. The number one sensor went off with a slow, steady but somewhat subdued beep, pause, beep, repeating itself. I alerted the crew. The number two sensor started beeping—a short two-beep signal, louder.

Then came number three, and when the four beeps in a row started in a loud, staccato pattern, I yelled, "Open Fire!"

And, open fire we did. It was pitch black; no one could see anything. Finally, after firing about 3000 rounds, we ceased firing and had no return fire. The next morning, we walked down the trail to retrieve our sensors and investigate what had caused this melee. To my chagrin, there was a dead water buffalo on the path, riddled by automatic weapons and machine gun fire. The premonition of an enemy attack, fear of the dark, and the evidence offered up by the seismic sensors had led me to waste 3000 rounds of ammunition, paid for by the American taxpayer, to kill a water buffalo. So how did I report this tale of mistaken identity? I knew that the Navy brass would not like a report that we had expended all of this ammunition in order to kill an animal on the loose, so I added to my report of the water buffalo fiasco that we estimated there were "two VC (KIA) probable." There was never any blowback from the Navy, but there probably would have been had only the water buffalo been reported. It wasn't a grand and glorious moment in my Navy career, yet, in retrospect, I probably did the practical thing. We would usually be down on the canal for three or four nights in a row setting up our ambush positions. We had enough hassle and worry going on without making a big deal of an innocuous gunfire report. So I fudged it. I had always doubted the accuracy of body counts and KIA reports. Now I knew why.

Probably the most well known boat for its Vietnam service was the Swift Boat. (It became especially prominent in the Presidential election of 2004.) At the western terminus of the Vinh Te Canal, at Ha Tien on the Gulf of Thailand, was a Navy Swift Boat base. The Swift Boat was larger than the PBR, had a bigger crew, was made of aluminum and had propellers (not jet pumps) for propulsion. It had a deeper draft than the PBR, was designed for patrolling coastal waters and was able to handle relatively rough ocean waters. In 1968 while considering volunteering for Vietnam and while on a ship that had stopped at Cam Ranh Bay, I went on a night patrol in a Swift boat to see what it was like. That patrol convinced me to volunteer for PBRs. All night that Swift Boat was pounded by the rough waves of the South China Sea. I had always been a seasick sailor, and by morning, I felt like I had spent a night in a washing machine. I was not interested in subjecting myself to that kind of agony so did not put "Swift Boat" in my requested transfer.

Since Swift Boats usually operated in deeper water, I hadn't seen much of them on the inland rivers of Vietnam until we got to the Vinh Te Canal. The western end of the waterway was generally deeper and wider. For the most part, the Swift Boats stayed at that end of the Canal. One day, I received orders to travel to Ha Tien to make contact with the Swift Boat base. There was also some indication that, with the monsoon ending and water levels expected to drop, PBRs might be taking over that end of the Canal for interdiction operations. I recall the day we took two PBRs down to Ha Tien, partially because it was such a beautiful, clear day, but also because of the manner in which I was introduced to another new technology.

There was a two-to-three-kilometer stretch of the Vinh Te Canal that defined the actual border between Vietnam and Cambodia. At the time, Americans were not supposed to be in Cambodia. (Later, in 1970, the President authorized an attack up the Mekong River into Cambodia.) But it was a gorgeous day, and the area we were transiting was a wide-open cow pasture with just a few trees along the bank on the Cambodian side. I said to the men: "Would anybody like to get their picture taken in Cambodia?" I think some of them were dumbfounded, but most of them, by then, knew that I was capable of such a thing. We pulled the boats over to the north side of the canal, got out and had our pictures taken. One of the crewmen was an African-American we called "Sarge." He was relatively new to the Division, and I had my photo taken with him standing in Cambodia. He had been in the Marine Corps and, through a strange set of circumstances, had transferred to the Navy. Because he had been a Marine, he was looked upon by our Navy men as a weapons expert. He knew how to set claymore mines, establish defensive positions, and lay out fields of fire—things that we Navy men really didn't know much about. He had also fired a weapon that we carried called a LAW (Light Anti-tank Weapon). It was like a bazooka, came in a case and, when unfolded, became a shoulder-fired rocket. It reminded me of the enemy's B-40 rocket launcher.

**ZIPPO FLAME THROWER WORKING ON VINH
TE CANAL, PBR PROVIDING COVER**

ZIPPO AT NIGHT, PHOTO BY JIM ROST

On this trip to Ha Tien, Sarge spotted a long, green cylinder hanging from a tree. We slowed the boat down to take a look at it. "Watch out for that!" he said. "It could be a booby trap." I had never seen anything like it, and he explained that it was a listening device that our intelligence people used to eavesdrop on the enemy. "It picks up people talking," he explained, "and transmits what they are saying to some headquarters command either in the Delta or up in Saigon." But he was doubtful about its location. "Usually, these are well hidden so that the enemy won't see them. This thing is right out here in the open, hanging under that tree. I wouldn't be surprised if it's booby-trapped."

What he said made a lot of sense to me. The listening device wasn't well camouflaged, and I thought that while we were there, we should destroy it. However, I didn't want to destroy something like this without prior approval. This was more than expending unneeded ammunition on a water buffalo. This electronic gizmo probably cost Uncle Sam $50,000. So I radioed our base and explained the situation. They checked with the Army, were told that there were no reported listening devices that had been set at that location, and that we should destroy it. Sarge pulled the LAW out of the case, unfolded it, and fired, putting a shot directly into the listening device. Nothing happened! I thought for sure that it would blow and that there would be some kind of secondary explosion, but— nothing. It was now full of holes and obviously unusable, so we left it hanging in the tree. A week or so later, we were told that it actually had been one of our listening devices, that it was in the right place, and that the Army had made a mistake in having us destroy it. So much for inter-service coordination; we did what we were told. This listening device was another technological breakthrough produced by the Vietnam War. There had also been cow tracks under it. It looked like cows used it to scratch their backs. Maybe they still do.

WITH SARGE IN CAMBODIA

*　*　*

This border interdiction operation needed supply bases and, again, the Navy came through with a vessel that was well suited for it. Our base for operations along the Vinh Te Canal was euphemistically called the YRBM-20. It was a 250-foot-long barge with a three-story, steel, box-like structure built on it that housed "Repair, Berthing and Messing" facilities. The top of the YRBM was flat so that it, too, could accommodate helicopters. There was a command, or Tactical Operations Center, (TOC) located right below the top deck. Like any barge, it could be towed, but for short movements it was equipped with what looked like monstrous outboard motor engines located on the stern. These were used daily to move the barge a mile or so up or down the Mekong River. It was not prudent to leave the YRBM in the same place each day and thereby entice the enemy to zero in on it from the shore.

For the PBR sailor, getting back to the YRBM-20 was always a welcome occasion. In its own ugly way, it was a "homey' place to be. Located near the City of Chau Doc, it was usually anchored near the middle of the big river and the shoreline seemed miles away, unlike the banks of the Vinh Te Canal, which were claustrophobic in their closeness. It felt safer being on the YRBM. Also, when we arrived on it, we could look forward to sleeping in air-conditioned spaces for two or three days. Officer's Country, where I stayed, was quite roomy and had a large wardroom with tables where we could play card games. There was a bunkhouse room for Patrol Officers. We didn't have our own stateroom so we would grab whichever bunk was available at the time. The sheets were always Navy-clean and, compared to living in your fatigues for three or four days out on patrol, they were a welcome experience. When we came in from patrol, we headed right for the sack for some well-deserved sleep.

YRBM 20

These stand-down days on the YRBM-20 also gave us a chance to meet other officers, catch up on the news and return to a semblance of normalcy. Larry Forbes, an officer with the tactical operations group on board, became a good friend. He had seen his own share of action at Muc Hoa, another area of the border interdiction operation. Today, he still remembers in detail the various commanders and Navy units that served along the Cambodian border. He, like many reserve officers, was willing to talk about the politics of the war as well as its execution. The wardroom of this ship-like barge was a place where you could connect your intellectual side with the emotions of living in and near a very dangerous place.

Navy men are always creative and those skills had been employed to their utmost on the YRBM. We all knew and had been trained that drinking on board ship in the U.S. Navy was not allowed. When beer was brought on board a Navy ship, it was always kept under lock and key, brought out only when a shore party could be arranged at some foreign port. The YRBM was not a ship; it was a barge, but the same rules applied. However, someone had figured out that a barge tied up next to a barge did not break these rules as long as the second barge was not Navy-owned. So some enterprising sailors found a barge, built a steel hooch on its deck, installed an air-conditioner, equipped it with a stereo and refrigerator and tied it up next to the YRBM-20. At 6 p.m. every night, a voice would come over the loud-speaker: "Beer Call! Beer Call!" Immediately, the officers and men living on the YRBM-20 would stream down a gangplank to the beer barge for happy hour.

It was an amazing example of Navy ingenuity at its best!

The beer barge and wardroom became a cultural melting pot. PBR sailors mixed with crews from the heavies, Vietnamese trainees became introduced to the taste of American beer, the brass (who were running the war) heard directly from those carrying out the operations, officers played bridge in the wardroom and critiqued the war (and each other) over a card game. Periodically, members of the press and official visitors from Saigon would arrive to assess what we were doing. It was a stimulating place to be in late 1969 if you were in Vietnam.

Not only were we training Vietnamese sailors and junior officers on our boats but, at the command level, more senior officers were involved. One of those officers, Thieu Ta (Lieutenant Commander) Lam, spoke excellent English and was very open in critiquing the war effort. He also was an accomplished bridge player and, when I was staying on the YRBM, we would often partner up in a card game. On 17 November 1969 (the same day that my friend, Jim Rost, was killed), in my Journal entry, I summarized Lam's comments on the war:

1. *"The war is about at the same place as it was two years ago. No significant improvement.*
2. *Democracy for Vietnam at this time is unrealistic and, in fact, is impossible.*
3. *There is a definite "feeling" between ethnic Chinese and Vietnamese in Vietnam; i.e. they don't get along.*
4. *There is widespread corruption in the government. Each man in position of leadership, "lines his own pockets" against the day when he may be out of a job.*
5. *The ACTOV program (our training of Vietnamese Navy personnel) is weak in that it is moving too fast and does not involve the training of enough boat captains and officers."*

It may have been an unintended consequence, but the YRBM became a home away from home. It was as if a little slice of America had been plopped down right in the middle of Vietnam. Most of the time, anchored out there in the middle of the Mekong River, it was hard to believe we were actually in a war zone. We knew that our friends, who were down on the canal just a few miles away, were right in the middle of it. But while we were on this floating platform which was our supply base, we pushed most of those concerns out of our thoughts. We could discuss the war not as active combatants, but almost as observers. Unfortunately, the further you stepped back from your own role, the bleaker the prospects looked for the future of what we were doing. A few days after recording Lam's observations, I had supper with Horst Faas of the Associated Press and wrote about it in my Journal. He and some other reporters had come down from Saigon to cover our operations on the Vinh Te Canal. It was another remarkable discussion about Vietnam while being in Vietnam.

"Last night we had a terrific discussion in the wardroom with Horst Faas of AP, a guy by the name of Walsh with Newsweek, and another guy from UPI. A Pulitzer Prize winner and a reporter in Vietnam for seven years, Faas has a tremendous grasp on the history of the war. His comment on the Vinh Te Canal: 'Whatever you guys do down in the Vinh Gia area will have no effect on the war. Traditionally, the Vietnamese have overlooked the area. They only care about the Canal as far down as the Seven Mountains. When the Americans leave, chances are no one will come in to take their place."

Horst Faas had voiced a perspective that I had not seen in any of the official reports related to our operations on the Vinh Te Canal. However, it was hard to argue against it when he knew the history of the country better than anyone I had yet met in Vietnam. His views also coincided with those of Bernard Fall and other authors who had written about the war. It became apparent that our border interdiction program would be a short-term operation, at least in this area. What looked on a map like a reasonable American Navy river operation was flying in the face of Vietnamese politics and history. (As I recall, in the conversation with Faas, Thieu Ta Lam also voiced similar views.) This knowledge imparted by a news reporter from Saigon had the opposite effect of "blowing someone up with a glory gun," yelling "Charge!" and then taking a hill. When I went back down on the Vinh Te Canal the next day for more nights of ambushes and patrols, I was scratching my head and asking,

"What are we doing this for?" But it was not a decision for me to make. The military works because it runs from the top down and everyone carries out orders. Discussions like this did have one recognizable effect—you stuck closer than ever to your friends and comrades and hoped that you would be the lucky one and dodge the next bullet.

LTJG LARRY FORBES ("THE L.A. KID")

Ten

Camping Out

Juxtaposed to the comforts of the YRBM 20 were the realities of our base camp at Vinh Gia on the Vinh Te Canal. Because the center of our operations along the Cambodian border was 40 or 50 miles away, the decision had been made to establish a base camp from which to operate. It took us three or four hours to make the trip. Had we been able to travel at top speed, it would have been much quicker, but the wake made by the PBR's when they were on step was a problem, especially in smaller canals. Imagine being on a quiet, serene lake in a canoe and then hearing the roar of 500 horsepower of boat engines followed by three-foot waves coming at you—that is what it was like when a PBR at top speed came rushing at you on a narrow canal. If you were in a small sampan you were going to be swamped. The Vinh Te Canal was the only highway to Vinh Gia, so we had to be careful to keep our speed down and respect others using the waterway. When heading for our base camp, we would usually start out in the morning, motor at low RPMs, and expect to arrive at our base camp by early afternoon.

CAMBODIA

MEKONG RIVER

CHAU DOC

VINH TE CANAL

BLOOD ALLEY

VINH GIA

SEVEN MOUNTAINS

HÁ TIÊN

VIETNAM

GULF OF THAILAND

VINH TE CANAL
SOUTH VIETNAM, 1969

One of the strange realities of the Vietnam War could be found at our favorite swimming hole. By day, it was a gorgeous site, a place to swim and relax. By night, it could be a hive of enemy gunfire.

The water in the Vinh Te Canal was, for the most part, of the typical Mekong Delta chocolate brown variety. You didn't want to drink from it, you wouldn't want to swim in it, but one of the pleasant surprises on this Canal was a turn-off about halfway to our base camp that we called "the French locks." When the French owned this territory, they had dredged a bypass and installed some locks to help navigate the Canal in low water. The locks were no longer working, but the bypass was still navigable and avoided the brown water current of the primary waterway. There was a pool between the locks where the water was calm, clear and deep—a natural swimming hole. Soon it became a regular stop on the way to our base camp at Vinh Gia. Guys would strip down to their shorts, dive in and then bask in the bright sunlight to cool off. At night, you could have firefights in the same place but, during the day, it was a beautiful place to go swimming.

Today the locks and the bypass are gone, but PBR sailors from 1969 would still know where to find the swimming hole. It was probably the best memory of the Vinh Te Canal.

Vinh Gia itself was a rather nondescript place. For most of the trip from the YRBM-20, the canal was bordered by rice fields on both sides. You passed a village called Tinh Bien, the main trading town in the area, and from it there was a connecting road to Cambodia. However, Vinh Gia itself wasn't large enough to be called a village—it was a widening in the dike line of the canal with a few houses located alongside. The Vietnamese military had built a small fort with a watchtower elevated above it. It was manned by about one hundred of their less reliable Regional and Provincial militia troops. It was, I believe, the presence of that outpost which prompted the Navy to make it a base camp for our operations. Looking at the fence and piles of sand bags that surrounded the outpost did not inspire confidence, but at least it provided a landmark on what was otherwise a flat, featureless part of the canal.

The heavies of River Assault Division 132 had preceded us in setting up the base camp, so there were already a bevy of Tango boats and other RAG boats on site when the PBRs arrived. The River Assault Division was led by an incredibly strong and able commander, Lieutenant Mike Connolly. Mike said that when his boats initially came in, one of them misjudged the current in the canal and took out a dock adjacent to the Vietnamese outpost. A tough fellow, Dai Uy (Captain) Doc, was the Army commander at the outpost. As Mike Connolly put it, "When we first went in there, one of our Monitors accidentally took out his wash pier. Doc said, 'Fix my God-damned pier!' I said, 'We'll fix it. Don't worry about it.' From then on, we were fine. He was my friend." Thus, we owed our good standing in the neighborhood to Mike's diplomatic skills. It was also comforting for the PBRs to have the heavies next to us. If the enemy did try to strike us here on the dike line of the Canal, we would have the beef and firepower of the RAG boats to back us up.

In describing the base camp, the most relevant word was "camp." There were a handful of buildings at the Vietnamese outpost, but there were none on the dike line where we beached our boats. The bank of the Canal was wide enough for us to stack supplies and for a helicopter to land but that was it. We lived on our boats at night while out on ambush positions, and we lived on them during the day back at the base camp. We cooked our own food or ate C-rations. The toilet was a barrel cut in half on a short section of dock which jutted out into the canal. If it rained, we put on a poncho or got under a boat canopy. This was our home for three or four days. We didn't change clothes, just wore more or fewer of them depending on the temperature. During the heat of the day, most of us wore just fatigue shorts and sandals. Nobody wore rank insignia unless it was camouflage black that couldn't be seen by the enemy. Since we were up most of the night, we tried to nap during the day. Unlike most camps, there were no volleyball or softball games—there was no room for a playing field on the dike line. Yet Vinh Gia was a camping experience in many respects: we were away from civilization, living out under the open sky, and had to depend on our campmates for safety and survival. The main difference from ordinary camping was our mission. We didn't sit around a campfire swapping stories. Rather, during the day, we hung around together trying to get a little sleep, reading mail, getting the guns greased, and making sure there was enough ammo for the next night's patrol.

From time to time, large Chinook helicopters came to the camp loaded with supplies, and they always had plenty of beer and bullets to drop off. I recall, on at least one occasion, requesting that they bring us some Coke or soft drinks. It was so hot we became dehydrated from the heat and, after awhile, beer didn't taste so good. We needed to have water and soft drinks.

On occasion, Chaplain Westling also came down to Vinh Gia by chopper to conduct a worship or memorial service. In another strange incongruence of war, we would pile up ammo cases to make an altar. The Chaplain was Episcopalian and so usually served communion as a part of the service. He was well liked and respected by the men. A slightly different attitude was felt toward the big wigs from Saigon who were running the war. When Admiral Zumwalt came down on Thanksgiving Day in a helicopter loaded with a hot, fresh turkey dinner, I had to roust out some of the PBR men to welcome him. "Why in the hell doesn't he come here at night," somebody said, "and then he would know what it is all about down on this canal." Yet in the end, out of respect for the Commander Naval Forces Vietnam (COMNAVFORV), everyone spruced up, combed his hair and put on a pair of pants and a fatigue shirt to welcome him. They all admitted after he left that, despite being where they were, it was one heck of a good Thanksgiving dinner. His visit also sent a message that the top brass knew about us, appreciated what we were doing and were, at least symbolically, tipping their hat to the men on the front line.

As our presence increased on the Vinh Te Canal, so did our contact with the enemy. My journal entry dated October 3, 1969, indicated that we were confronting not only male soldiers but female. A firefight on October 1st was with some Viet Cong women. The fight took place between them and the RAG boats (call sign "Brass Rail"). Because the water was still high, the heavies were supported by air boats similar to what you would find in the Florida Everglades. They had a two-man crew:

helmsman/driver in the rear and a very exposed forward gunner in the bow manning a .30 caliber machine gun. During high water they could zip along at high speeds over the flooded rice fields of the area. These boats had been assigned an American Army Advisor but were manned by South Vietnamese soldiers of Chinese descent. (Reminiscent of America's treatment of black soldiers in World War II, Vietnamese, who were ethnically of Chinese descent, were not allowed to fight in regular Vietnamese Army units during the Vietnam War.)

"Just completed four patrols on the Vinh Te. At 0300 on 1 October, 'Brass Rail Whiskey' saw a sampan crossing and opened up. Shot up an illumination flare and saw two more. Brought the "Black Ponies" in for a strike. VN troops made a sweep along with their airboats. Results four VC/ NVA KIA and four probable. Two Chicoms (Chinese Communist rifles), 1 AK-47 and one .50 cal. machine gun captured. The enemy were all women—a logistics company from Ha Tien going into Cambodia for supplies. One of them opened up with an AK-47 at an airboat. He hit her with a .30 cal. machine gun. With her stomach opened, she still walked two kilometers to an outpost to get medical help before she died.

Militarily, the operation was conducted well. 'Brass Rail Whiskey' did the right thing on the scene and Mike Connolly did a superb job coordinating from Vinh Gia. It was combatant against combatant. No civilians killed."

By the second week of October, the Navy had decided to put more boats on the Vinh Te Canal. Later, orders would be issued to have the PBRs separate from their cover boats in order to set up more ambush positions along the Canal. These changes were made to give the Navy better coverage of potential enemy crossing points, but it separated us from the protection usually provided by a cover boat. Also, it meant even longer patrols and more hours on the canal. I wrote about it in the journal, and also complained about it to the Commanding Officer of the operation.

> *"On 05 October, CTG 194.4 (Commander Task Group), 'Company Store,' directed that all River Divisions put seven boats a day on the river. This order supposedly came down from COMNAVFORV (Admiral Zumwalt) who is trying to build his PBR 'curtain' to stop infiltration along the border. That means that boats and crews could be 'on the river' 120-144 hours per week. It is going to mean tired crews and limited reaction time in night ambushes. I wrote a Memo to Commander Storms bitching about it, but it probably won't do much good."*

The night after this order came out, I wrote of another encounter between the RAG boats and the enemy which lasted about thirty minutes, and the morning search had found "numerous blood trails going into Cambodia." Interestingly, the PBRs, on the same night, had set up a position right in the middle of Vinh Gia. We had no contact with the enemy, but I wrote of some interesting things that happened that night. There was a dusk-to-dawn curfew for all boat traffic, and the assumption was that any boat moving was doing so illegally and probably up to no good. In this case, there was a legitimate reason for a boat we saw. Fortunately, there was no accident.

> *"While all of the action with RAG boats was going on, we chased a sampan that was crossing near us. Result: one pregnant woman going to a maternity clinic. I fired what I had been told was*

> *an M-79 illumination grenade. Instead, it was a*
> *fragmentation grenade. Fortunately, I put it into*
> *a rice paddy and no one was hurt. Since we were*
> *close to town, I overheard an argument between*
> *a man and his wife. According to our Vietnamese*
> *crewmen, he was drunk and wanted to take her to*
> *bed. She didn't like the idea, and they were having*
> *quite a screaming session. War certainly is a strange*
> *mixture."*

The constant and nearly continual night patrol duties took their toll. I found that men were more alert and better prepared if we staggered watches at night, providing for at least some sleep. Then, on October 15 I recorded what may have been my closest call to being killed in Vietnam.

I had scheduled myself for a nap at about midnight when there was a rocket attack. One of my favorite places to lie down was on top of the boat canopy, which acted as a kind of hammock.

> *"At 0030, the VC shot at our cover boat with a*
> *107 mm rocket. They missed and it went about*
> *thirty feet over our boat. I had just lain down on*
> *the canopy to sleep. All of a sudden this tremendous*
> *VROOM as it exploded. Cover boat opened fire*
> *and moved. We illuminated. Sea Wolves and Black*
> *Ponies put in strikes. Then we put in some H &*
> *I (harassment and interdiction) with our .60 mm*
> *mortar. Sweep at dawn—negative results. Lesson*
> *learned—there is no alarm clock like a 107 mm*
> *rocket going over your head!"*

My memory of that experience is that the rocket, as it went over the boat, had a swooshing sound, like it was tumbling through the air. It detonated harmlessly on the opposite bank of the canal.

In retrospect, it is hard to describe the need for sleep under those conditions. You would think that the tension and fear of attack would produce so much adrenalin that you couldn't even think of sleeping, but that wasn't the case. After long patrols lasting several days, you felt as if you were running on what we called "electrical energy." In the job we were doing and the hours involved, you needed to have a super reserve of energy to keep going. Yet men are mammals and, ultimately, need sleep. Despite the close call on October 15, I wrote a week later in the journal:

"I slept right through a terrific thunderstorm last night. Fell asleep under a poncho on the engine cover. Woke at 0500 with one side of me all wet—couldn't figure out what had happened. Some indication of how tired you get."

As the month of October progressed, so did the fighting. The RAG boats had taken over major responsibility for the canal west of Vinh Gia, an area we called "blood alley." On two consecutive nights, I recorded heavy fighting between the heavies and the enemy. I described the results as a "depressing example of what war is all about."

> *"October 20th: In the early hours of the morning, a Tango boat got three sampans crossing at approximately the 64 N/S gridline. Greased two, one made it to the north bank. Next morning I took two RAG boat types (men) to lead a sweep. Arrived at 0730, started searching, sampan captured, four documents and a B-40 rocket.*
>
> *At the same time, VN troops started sweeping the north bank for the other sampan. There was a tremendous explosion—wood, arms, legs, and bodies flying in all directions. Charlie had booby-trapped this second sampan with a command-detonated mine. A really horrible, gory scene as*

> *the remaining VN troops gathered the completely*
> *dismembered bodies of their friends."*

In retrospect, this tragedy could probably have been avoided had the Vietnamese troops been more cautious in their search for the sampan. However, they were motivated to find weapons. If they brought back enemy rifles or weapons, they would receive a bonus at their next payday. It was a system that rewarded them, but it could also lead to careless search procedures like the one that I had just witnessed.

The next day, October 21, the RAG boats were at it again. This time they caught a large contingent of North Vietnamese and Viet Cong in the open rice fields between the Vinh Te Canal and the Cambodian border. A South Vietnamese Army unit had set up an ambush site on the Cambodian border, discovered this enemy force and called in the coordinates to our Navy RAG boats. I have often wondered if this ambush was set to retaliate for the prior day's killing of South Vietnamese troops with the booby-trapped sampan, but that is something we will never know.

> *"Charlie attempted a major crossing from the north*
> *at the #67 N/S grid line, supported by troops on the*
> *south bank. This 150 man VC force was discovered*
> *by a "friendly" ambush set up at the Cambodian*
> *border. A Monitor 105 mm 'arty' with bee hive*
> *rounds hit directly in the enemy position, making*
> *bodies unrecognizable. Helo and Black Pony*
> *strikes put in. 11 VC KIA, 7 probable, 5 AK-47's*
> *captured. So the war goes on—first one side and*
> *then the other."*

My diary entry for 25-28 October, 1969, was very brief:

> *"Three days Vinh Te Canal—firefight by RAG*
> *boats—on tape."*

I can only presume that the brevity of this entry reflects exhaustion. I was so tired when I got back to the YRBM that I went right to sleep after writing just a few words. The entry mentioned "tape." I had taken a tape recorder with me on patrol a couple of times to record the radio traffic. I had it with me on October 26 when, early in the evening, the heavies were attacked en route to their night ambush positions along "blood alley." I later gave copies to some of my friends on the YRBM. The tape is worth listening to and vividly describes the chaos and emotion of a group of American RAG boats being ambushed on the Vinh Te Canal. Something else happened which, at the time, I knew nothing about. The tape apparently got to an Admiral at headquarters who was directly responsible for the Navy border interdiction operation. Mike Connolly had been very prominent on the radio the night of the engagement in commanding and coordinating the RAG boat response to the ambush. One day, when Mike was at Navy headquarters in Binh Thuy, he was ordered to see the Admiral. He felt trepidation because he had no idea of why he had been called in. According to Mike, the Admiral "was kind of a stern-looking guy, and I walked in and stood at attention. He said, 'What do you think of this?' Then he played part of that tape. I tried to dodge the question, thinking he might be going to chew me out. Then he slapped his knee and said: 'I think it's great, and I've got a copy for you!'" Mike went on to become one of the most highly decorated officers of the Brown Water Navy.

By early November, 1969, the fighting on the Vinh Te Canal had become nearly continuous. More men were being killed, including the Vietnamese we were training whom we referred to as "friendlies." Our well-liked River Division C.O., Ron Lepak, who was always calm and cool about things, was even showing the strain of war. On November 13th, I wrote this entry in the Journal.

> *"Last night was a bad one for the RAG boats. About four of them got hit with B-40's. Two VN's were killed and three or four injured.*

125

People are on edge all along the canal because of the rise in activity. This is the fourth, "friendly" KIA in just over a week. As the water goes down due to the end of the monsoon season, we will probably continue to get a lot of action.

Ron Lepak came down the canal two days ago, and was showing signs of combat fatigue: nervousness, tired, jumpy. After a few days back on the YRBM he seemed better. But this is an example of how many are feeling. We had been primarily stopping the VC supply people. Now they've brought in the NVA (North Vietnamese) to try and push through. The enemy is 'gutsy,' that's for sure."

It had been nearly two months since I made the euphoric false prediction that there would be very little happening on Vinh Te Canal. It is clear from my journal that during this time, it was the RAG boats that took the most punishment. However, that would soon change. The monsoon was over, and the water level in the Canal was dropping. It wouldn't be long before there would no longer be enough water in the canal to float the heavy, steel-armored boats. PBRs required less water depth. It was evident that we would be staying in the canal to continue these operations; no one was enthusiastic about that prospect. The low water had already begun to diminish the effectiveness of the PBRs' automatic weapons. As the water dropped, we had to angle our guns up to clear the dike lines, and in many places we couldn't see what was on the other side of the banks. To adjust for this at night, in our ambush positions, we began putting a couple of men on top of the canal bank with an M-60 machine gun so that we could have a field of fire. Now I better understood why men in the infantry liked to have tanks around. The RAG boats were our "tanks," and they would be pulling out when the water dropped to a level where their propellers started hitting bottom. Their departure was not something that we looked forward to.

BASE CAMP IN VINH GIA

SWIMMING AT THE FRENCH LOCKS

OUT HOUSE AT VINH GIA

BASE CAMP READING MAIL, VINH GIA, VINH TE CANAL, 1969

128

CHAPLAIN WESTLING AT VINH GIA

LIVE AIRSTRIKE AUDIO RECORDING FROM VINH TE CANAL, 1969.

SCAN CODE TO LISTEN (*http://goo.gl/atxkzG*)

––––––––

00.15 / The first part of this tape is a re-recording of an OV-10 Bronco air strike on the Vinh Te Canal. I am listening to and recording the events of a previous night when a PBR boat captain had recorded the sounds of this air strike. He and I are laughing and commenting on what occurred. At one point, a siren goes off, the signal to stop firing. Then a Vietnamese sailor yells at a local outpost for them to cease firing. The outpost had been firing mortars into an area where these Navy strike aircraft (with the call sign "Black Pony") were flying. From the tape, you can hear metal shell casings falling on the deck of the PBR as the machine guns are fired. Tracers from PBR machine guns were often used to support air strikes by marking the location of enemy positions. The sound of the twin engine OV-10's can be heard as they fly low over the boat on their strafing runs toward the target.

04.15 / On October 26, 1969, I tape-recorded the radio traffic during an enemy attack against our heavy River Assault Group boats. The position of our PBR was about a mile from the encounter. We could see the firefight in the distance. The call sign for the RAG boat commander was "Brass Rail", and individual boats under attack are designated by various letters of the phonetic alphabet. U.S. Navy Seawolf helicopters and fixed wing Black Pony attack aircraft can also be heard calling in. A RAG boat radio sometimes remains keyed in the "on" position and you can hear yelling and firing in the background. The tape accurately describes the chaos, anxiety and fear experienced in a firefight.

––––––––

Eleven

Engineer

Jim Rost and I had a lot in common, but one important difference: he chose his words carefully and listened before speaking. I tended to immediately engage in conversation, even if I should have been quiet. Fortunately, this difference didn't prevent us from becoming good friends.

Jim was an engineer with a college degree from the Stevens Institute of Technology in Hoboken, N.J. He was tall and slim with a terrific smile. I got to know him in the wardroom at the YRBM, but he was not a PBR sailor; he was an operations officer with the RAG boats. One thing that drew Jim Rost and me together was our background in theology. Jim had been in a pre-seminary program at a Catholic high school on Long Island. He had pursued a course of study taken by those going into the priesthood, while I had studied at a Methodist seminary in Illinois; neither of us would enter the Christian ministry. It was never clear to me what had changed Jim's mind, but this common link in our studies often ended up in our conversations.

His background in engineering school had followed him into the Navy. His goal was to become a Main Propulsion Assistant (MPA) on a Destroyer. I never had much interest in engineering, but my brother did. He had graduated in engineering from

Purdue University and had become an MPA in the Navy. It was an important job in the Engineering Department of any ship with responsibility for the engine room and propulsion system. Being an engineer seemed to be in Jim Rost's blood. His brothers, David and Paul, had also graduated from Stevens in engineering. Paul, in a written personal memoir entitled "My Brother Jimmy," explained that "the fact that all three of the Rost boys became engineers should not be surprising." Their father had studied engineering but had dropped out of engineering school to take a job in banking. "But," as Paul wrote, "he always had a strong interest in how things worked and passed that on to us. He had a microscope and showed us bacteria, blood cells and other stuff under slides. He taught us photography, and how to develop, print and enlarge photos; and he urged and allowed us to explore these interests on our own." The inquisitive side that I saw in Jim Rost had come through his being in a family of engineers.

There was another interest Jim had that I didn't. He loved the Navy.

I liked the Navy, but I didn't love it. I couldn't see myself staying in and making a career of it, but he often expressed his interest in the sea, boats, ships and what made them go. I remember predicting to him that he would stay in the Navy. I just couldn't see him outside of it. A part of his being quiet included his patience. The bureaucracy and paperwork of the Navy drove me crazy. He didn't particularly like it, but he could accept it. He had an attitude and demeanor that looked at the big picture and didn't get bogged down in the day-to-day. Had he decided to pursue a Navy career, I think he would have set his sights on being the Commanding Officer of a Frigate or a Destroyer and never looked back.

Jim was also a deep thinker, not ponderous or boring. He was smart. You knew that he was interested in what was below the surface as well as what was visible on top. Some Navy men shied away from talking about religion and politics, but not Jim Rost. He had one of those inquisitive personalities, often seen in engineers, that always wants to find out what is on the other side of the horizon. So when we were together on the YRBM-20, at happy hour, we would seek out the same table at the beer barge and start talking. Like others I met in Vietnam, I didn't know him long, just a couple of months, but I can still visualize the end of the day and looking forward to hearing about what this man had been thinking since the last time we talked. It was a friendship which I knew would survive the war. Whether he stayed in the Navy or didn't, Jim Rost and I would be staying in touch and corresponding.

So it was not easy the night that he was killed on the Vinh Te Canal. It happened to be on a night when I wasn't on patrol. I was sitting in the air-conditioned wardroom of the YRBM-20 playing bridge when the news came in.

November 17, 1969:

It will be hard to get to sleep. LTJG Jim Rost was killed tonight in a B-40 ambush on the Vinh Te. We were sitting there in the wardroom on the YRBM playing bridge. The opposition had just made a 3 no-trump bid and made rubber. Commander Storms, with my help, had been steadily losing. The word came in on the attack and he had to leave. Bob Farr filled in, but our minds were no longer on bridge.

The movie was a complete bust. Gina Lollobrigida, Peter Lawford, and the guy who used to play "Bilko" on T.V. It was a poor comedy and made even more tasteless by the tragedy we had just heard about from Vinh Gia. By the second reel, word had come of one killed and several wounded. By the third reel, the buzzer blatted three times for the second "dust-off" (medical evacuation helicopter) coming in with wounded.

I wrote off the movie along with everyone else. We stood in silence below the flight deck of the YRBM 20, bending into the strong wind and watching a storm move in. The helo appeared out of the overcast heading in from Nui Sam Mountain, fought its way to the deck in the wind and touched down. A flurry of activity—all in silence—as stretchers moved with speed and ease from the helicopter, down the incline to sickbay. Shortly thereafter, two seriously wounded VNs, having been treated temporarily by Doc Stank, were shuttled on up to the waiting bird for evacuation to the Long Xuyen hospital.

In an air of unreality, we all made ourselves busy—reading, playing solitaire, shining shoes— waiting for the confirmation of the KIA. At 2230 I went up to the NOC (Naval Operations Center) to see if there was any more word from Vinh Gia, and it was coming in then on the radio. Jim had been killed, his remains to be flown to Binh Thuy in the morning. Dufflebag sensors (snooping devices) were needed to cover the ambush area, a helo was needed in the morning, etc. In a sort of sordid monotony, the war drones on. We all felt the impact of Jim's death; but, in our own way, we trudged along our separate paths not denying but only camouflaging our despair.

Commander Storms was efficient and decisive but he too showed the strain of battle. An air-conditioned operations center doesn't shield one from that. I noted, with new respect, the burden of responsibility that only a military commander can know.

Jim Rost was quiet. I remember him talking about the Navy a lot. He loved it—an engineering grad caught up in the technicalities of steam plants and engineering things. He thought he might stay in the Navy. He was an unassuming guy you would probably pass without noticing; but out on the river, he was doing his job. Far from being a lover of war, you would more likely have found him ushering in Church on a Sunday morning. His loss will be with us forever, though the depth of the wound can be known only by his family. Such incidents seem to cloud reality and tonight was a night of that."

This was the longest entry of my Vietnam Journal. It was obvious I hadn't slept much that night and stayed up writing. It was an even tougher night for Jim's commanding officer, Mike Connolly. As Mike told me: "The night of 17 November is always a difficult evening for me. Jim was a gem and the day he was killed remains one of the worst days of my life." From time to time, on the anniversary of that night, Mike has sponsored a Memorial Mass in Jim's name at his home church in Malverne, New York. He has also laid a wreath in his name at the Vietnam Wall. One recent year, he spoke of Jim Rost during a wreath-laying ceremony at the Navy Memorial. For Mike Connolly, the memories of November 17, 1969, have never gone away.

When I met Mike Connolly to interview him about Jim Rost, he suggested, "Let's meet at the Mekong Restaurant in Richmond." Could there be a place with a more perfect name? We hadn't seen each other since the Mekong Delta in 1970. I was visiting my daughter in Washington, D.C. and Mike lives in Lynchburg, Virginia, so we met halfway at this Vietnamese Restaurant for lunch. For those who knew Mike Connolly in Vietnam, he is much the same today. He walks with a confident stride, is unpretentious and speaks from his heart. We started our conversation with my telling him of finding Chief Tozer's daughters in Michigan and then his sister in Quebec. Because Mike had been the senior commander at the base camp in Vinh Gia, he had also assumed tactical control of PBR operations there. He had known Eldon Tozer through that relationship, and had been at the base camp the night Chief Tozer died. He had tried to comfort the Chief as he was dying. "As I recall," Mike said, "the Chief said to me, 'I can't die.' I found out later why— because his wife had already died and he needed to stay alive for his kids."

So there we were in a Vietnamese Restaurant in Richmond, Virginia forty years later, speaking about men we had known who were killed in Vietnam. I had forgotten about Mike's sense of humor. When I asked him if he were a graduate of the Naval Academy at Annapolis, he replied, "Oh, no. I have a real college degree!" We both laughed. Mike had gone to the University of Minnesota and then to Officer Candidate School (OCS) in Newport, R.I. It was the same route (from university to OCS) that Jim Rost and I had taken when we joined the Navy. Jim and I had volunteered to go to Vietnam, but, on the issue of volunteering, Mike was clear that he had gone because of orders.

"I didn't volunteer," he said. "I was 29 and had two children. When I got the orders, I called the Bureau of Naval Personnel, and they said: 'You should be very happy. We only pick the top ten percent for this.' I said, 'I'm overjoyed! I'm not going to try and weasel out, but please give me a good job. Give me something that is at least career-enhancing.' And I got a good job—though, at the time, I don't think the detailers thought so.

Later, when Admiral Zumwalt became CNO (Chief of Naval Operations), they did give more credit for combat experience."

When LT Connolly went to Vietnam, he was assigned as Commanding Officer of River Assault Division 132. "At first," he said, "we were working with the Army." As a part of the Mobile Riverine Force, the RAG boats transported troops, usually from the 9th Infantry Division, and inserted them into combat operations. "When they released us from the Army," Mike continued, "they sent us to Moc Hoa as a part of Operation Giant Slingshot, around the Parrot's Beak border area with Cambodia. We kind of earned a good reputation up there with some of the PBR groups because we were big enough to slug it out and help them."

I told Mike that as far as I was concerned, the RAG boats had more than "kind of earned" that reputation. They paid for it dearly, with the lives of men like Jim Rost.

Jim had gone through Survival School with Mike Connolly back in the States but operationally, in Vietnam, they had worked somewhat independently from each other until their unit's assignment to the Vinh Te Canal. According to Mike, "Jim had gone down on the Canal just a few days before he was killed. He was the number-three guy in our outfit. Our Chief of Staff was back on the YRBM." Because action was heating up on the Canal, Jim was sent down to Vinh Gia to help Mike Connolly, who was not only coordinating the operation but was also going out on patrols.

In describing the demeanor of Jim Rost, Mike used a quotation from Mark Twain: He had the quiet calm "of a Christian with four aces." Jim's commander saw in him the characteristics of a natural leader. "Jim wanted to go out on the boats even when there was no requirement for an officer to be along. He didn't like sitting in the command boat back at the base, but preferred getting out and about."

Mike added, "Most telling was the absolute pall that fell over our Division when he was killed. He had, in a short time, earned the respect and brotherly love of his comrades."

In our discussions on Chief Tozer, I told Mike that through the luck of the draw, I had been spared the night the Chief was killed. I had originally been scheduled to be the Patrol Officer at the location where he was hit. Instead, I had stayed back at the base camp in Vinh Gia to learn more about coordinating helicopter and air support. It was going to become the role of the PBRs to assume command as well as patrol functions once the water levels got too low for the heavies. I told Mike that I had similar feelings about Jim Rost's death.

"I felt that when Jim was killed, that it probably should have been me," I said. "He was driving what was the equivalent of a tank, and I was on a boat built more like a jeep." The chances of a B-40 rocket making a direct and fatal hit on a RAG boat seemed less likely to me than taking the same hit on an unarmored PBR.

Mike Connolly told me that, originally, he had been scheduled to go out on patrol instead of Jim. "The night he was killed, he was on a Tango boat. I was supposed to go out on that patrol. Until he was killed, I was going out a lot. When the word was originally received at the YRBM that an officer had been killed, they thought it was me."

The happenstance of war, the vagaries of it, are sometimes harder to understand than the realities of it. Both Mike Connolly and I were alive because of unplanned and unexpected changes in our schedules.

"They apparently forgot that Jim had just recently come down to Vinh Gia to help take the strain off me," Mike said. "I guess I was feeling the strain, going out almost every night and then trying to organize things during the daytime. So he went out on that boat and was sitting where the officer in charge sits—where I would have been."

For Mike Connolly, Jim Rost's death also resulted in a change of policy which removed him at least one step from being exposed to hostile fire. "The day after Jim was killed," Mike explained, "Commander Storms flew in and ordered me to 'stay off the boats going out on patrol. You stay in Vinh Gia on the Command Boat,' he said." Though there were no guarantees of safety at the small, relatively unprotected base camp, the Navy didn't want to risk losing their Senior Commander on the Vinh Te Canal to another B-40 rocket attack while on a boat heading for an ambush position.

In our conversation, I mentioned to Mike that I had traveled to Malverne, New York, on Long Island, to meet with Jim Rost's siblings. While there we talked about his funeral. The funeral didn't take place until December 1ˢᵗ, and the family thought there may have been some delay in having the body transported home. However, Mike's memory was that Jim's remains were flown out the next morning, and he expected that they would be returned to the States in a timely fashion. David Rost, Jim's brother, told me that the front of the casket was open and visible and that Jim's head had what looked like a skull cap on it. Mike observed: "Yes, it was a direct hit on the back of his head that killed him, and he also had heavy shoulder damage." If there is any comfort for his family, it is at least clear that Jim Rost was killed instantly. He did not linger or suffer in death.

Mike Connolly had, and still has, a wonderful relationship with the men who served under him. He was one of them. Since ending his career in the Navy, Mike has taught history in college and, over the years, students have asked him, "What was it like? Did you kill anyone?" "My response to them," Mike explained, "is that over there I found out how to love a brother. Although I actually had a brother much younger than myself, we weren't that close. But my experience in Vietnam taught me to love another man. I'd never really had that before. I wasn't very close to my father either."

At this point in our conversation, I made a comment reflecting what I thought Mike was getting at. "It was an enforced fraternity in a way," I said. Yet it was more than that for Mike Connolly. He truly did love the men who served under his command.

"Oh, there were some scruffy devils in that outfit," he admitted, "but I would have gone anywhere with them or for them." In every war there is camaraderie spawned by loyalty to one's combat unit. It has led some, as perhaps it did Chief Tozer, to return to their units though they were eligible for a transfer to peacetime duty. But Mike Connolly was saying something more; there was something deeper here. Men can love one another enough to be absolutely committed to each other's well being. It was true in 1969 along the Cambodian border on the Vinh Te Canal.

Mike and I also talked about our views on the Vietnam War. I was obviously more circumspect about its viability at that time than he was. "I grew up in a very conservative family, but I attended a very liberal university where I was turned off, honestly, by some of the anti-war rhetoric," he explained. "I was pretty conservative. I think when the demonstrations in the States started, that pushed me into being more defensive about the war. A lot of the opponents to the war were people who didn't go into the service or who ran to Canada, so part of my feelings were related to that. Now, though, as I look back,

I can see that a lot of horrible mistakes were made relative to Vietnam."

This part of conversation quickly came to a close. Such speculation on the causes and justice of a war now seem like an asterisk on a footnote. What was driving our reunion over lunch were our memories of the men we knew and the experiences we shared.

Our conversation returned to Jim Rost, who he was and what he had been writing prior to his death. I showed Mike correspondence that Jim had written to his sister, Mary, and his brother-in-law, Jim, on 23 September 1969. It is an extensive letter and nearly half of it is taken up with how the Brown Water Navy was organized and the various number designations given to Task Forces (TF), Task Groups (TG) and Task Units (TU). He wrote, "Right now I'm in TG 194.4. A week ago I was in TG 194.7."

"As far as I'm concerned," I expressed to Mike, "that shows he had a deep interest and curiosity in the chain-of-command and how it worked." It was one of the reasons I believed Jim Rost would likely follow a Naval career. Mike can't recall ever having a definitive talk with Jim about whether or not he would stay in the Navy, yet he remembers the qualities that made him a good Naval Officer. "I don't ever remember him being negative about anything. He was very orderly and really took care of his troops. They all loved him."

I informed Mike that Jim had specifically requested his assignment to RAG boats. "His brother has the personnel records indicating that he had volunteered for Vietnam and requested operations in a River Assault Group. He got what he wanted." To me, the evidence is strong that had Vietnam worked out for him, Jim Rost would have decided to remain in the U.S. Navy.

There is another letter from Jim Rost that I shared with Mike—a letter describing the base camp at Vinh Gia which was sent to a Mrs. Bell, his brother's mother-in-law. In that letter, written nine days before his death, Jim disputed my conclusions about his staying in the Navy: "I still don't really know what I'll do when I get back. I'll probably get out of the Navy and spend a few weeks looking for a job," he wrote to Mrs. Bell. Would he really have left the Navy? Somehow, I still doubt that. His letter describes the fighting on the Vinh Te Canal as "quite light. We've had several people wounded but no one killed. These boats show an amazing ability to absorb damage and keep on going." Yet, he knew, and we all knew, that things were heating up. The Navy, as we knew it from having served on ships, was not what we were experiencing along this canal that bordered Cambodia. Could the Vinh Te Canal operation have thrown some cold water on his Navy plans? We will never know.

Mike Connolly was speechless when he read the words that Jim wrote about him: "My boss is one of the friendliest and most diplomatic people around. He has managed to get excellent cooperation from the Vietnamese base commander. My boss has been making quite a name for himself. As far as the Navy is concerned, this is the hottest area in Vietnam right now. We have a lot of VIP's coming through." All of this was true, of course, and Mike readily admitted that "Vietnam made my career in the Navy." It also didn't hurt that his leadership skills came to be recognized by Admiral Zumwalt, Commander Naval Forces Vietnam (COMNAVFORV), who would later become CNO, the Chief of Naval Operations for the U.S. Navy. Jim Rost's views of his commanding officer square with what I had seen and experienced myself. Mike Connolly was the kind of commander who would not ask you to do anything he was not ready to do or had not already done.

This letter to Mrs. Bell also voiced support for political efforts to end the War. Jim started his letter by saying: "Well, today,

I'm more than half way home. Less than six months to go. And we can hope for the President to bring us home earlier." Later, in the letter, he wrote: "I listened to the President's November 3rd speech and I must say that I agree 100% with him." In a speech called "The Silent Majority," President Nixon had made it clear that plans for "Vietnamizing" the War were going forward and that American troop withdrawals from the country would continue. The President articulated a new reality: the citizens of the United States were tired of the war and public opinion had turned against it. In an earlier letter to his family, Jim had expressed sentiments that echoed those of his President. He had asked a Vietnamese Navy Lieutenant whom he was training about what he would do when the War ended. "Get out and teach," the man said. According to Jim, "Most of the people here are of the opinion we are pulling out come hell or high water. And that is the best thing to do."

Jim Rost was doing his job in Vietnam, but he knew that there was an end coming to U.S. military involvement there. He just never lived long enough to see it.

In reading Jim Rost's letter to Mrs. Bell, I learned of an event that occurred on the Vinh Te Canal that I had not known about. "The past few nights we've been observing a helicopter flying over Cambodia," he wrote. "One night it flew into South Vietnam. We have some OV-10 Broncos that are just itching to shoot it down. We figure they're using it to try to spot our ambush positions to figure out where they can get through. Intelligence says they have fifteen tons of supplies they're trying to bring across. That's a lot of sampan loads." Jim didn't finish the story in this letter, but Mike Connolly did. When I asked Mike about the helicopter snooping at night from Cambodia, he said: "We shot it down. Shot it down with a .50 cal. He would come over, see a boat, go back—and that boat would then get mortared. I think I told Storms [his immediate commander] what I was going to do, and he said, 'OK, just be sure it falls in Cambodia!' And it did. We dropped it." We both laughed.

It was hard to end this remarkable lunch that I had with Mike Connolly. We knew each other only a few months in Vietnam, but it was as if we had never left. We had talked for two hours about events that seemed like yesterday but which had occurred forty years ago.

Mike still sometimes wakes up at night thinking about Jim Rost.

"The night he was killed, I sat up all night with Dai Uy Doc in the little gazebo where his body had been wrapped by Vietnamese nurses," Mike said.

Grey Wrather, the Navy corpsman assigned to River Assault Division 132, also remembered that long night of vigil over Jim Rost's body. "As I remember it," Wrather recounted, "the South Vietnamese commander brought in two women who lived in or near the outpost and who were skilled at preparing bodies. It is the Vietnamese tradition to honor the deceased by washing the body and then wrapping it in a white, muslin cloth. Mike Connolly told Dai Uy Doc that all of this work would probably be altered by the Navy once Jim's body got back to a U.S. base in the morning. But the Dai Uy responded, 'That is OK. This is our tradition of properly caring for the dead. We should do this now.'" After the women had prepared the body, they dressed Jim in a fresh fatigue uniform. Mike Connolly, Doc Wrather and Dai Uy Doc stayed up through the night with Jim's body and waited for the sun to come up. A helicopter was scheduled to arrive shortly after dawn and begin the journey of Jim Rost's return to the United States.

"It still haunts my memories," Mike Connolly told me. "He was evacuated in the morning, and I can still see that helicopter disappearing in the distance with him."

On November 18, 1969, the day after his death, Mike Connolly wrote Jim Rost's mother a personal letter and sent with it an American flag that had flown from the RAG boats on the Vinh Te Canal. The letter speaks for itself from the heart of a Commander who had just lost a friend, colleague and respected leader. Also, I am sure, it reflected the feelings of all who knew or had met Jim Rost in Vietnam when he served in the Brown Water Navy with River Assault Division 132.

DEPARTMENT OF THE NAVY
COMMANDER RIVER ASSAULT DIVISION-132
FPO San Francisco, California 96601

Mrs. J. F. Rost   November 18, 1969
65 Home Street
Malverne, New York

Dear Mrs. Rost,

I write to convey my personal condolences and those of the officers and
men of River Assault Division 132 in the recent loss of your son, Jim.
No words of mine, I know, can assuage the grief you must feel, but I
trust that the courageous and honorable memories we have of your son will
serve to give you proud remembrance of him.

Jim died at 7:02 P. M. on the night of 17 November. He was serving as
patrol officer for a group of boats on the Vinh Te Canal along the
Cambodian border. The boats had often been attacked in this area and Jim
volunteered to ride with the boats to give leadership to the group and
to reassure them in the face of enemy attacks without warning. On
previous occasions, he had shown unfaltering courage when under fire and
earned the respect of every man in our division. When the attack commenced,
Jim called on the radio to tell me where he was and shortly thereafter
was struck down by enemy fire. Jim died instantaneously; he had no
warning, he knew no pain. His last actions in reporting his position and
in personally returning fire were calm and deliberate selfless actions to
best defend and support the men under his command.

As you may already know, Jim and I went through training at Mare Island
together, then joined the Division together. In my prior association with
Naval officers, I have respected some and liked others. Jim was the rare
combination of sincerity and decency which one respects as well as likes.
His quiet yet deliberate manner and his genuine concern for his subordinates
drew many friends and earned him a special respect among the sailors in
our division as well as the men from other divisions with which we worked.

As Jim so often spoke warmly of his family and of happy family memories,
I know that this must be a time of deep anguish for you and your children.
Men from all of the boats here with me have asked if there was something
they might do or some appropriate way they might convey to you their
deepest sympathies. They asked that I forward to you the American Flag
which is the "special occasions" flag for our division. It has flown from
the masts of River Assault craft on many proud occasions. I hope you will
accept it in the sincere spirit in which it is offered. It will be
enclosed with Jim's personal effects which should be delivered to you
within 30 days.

Though Jim has passed from among us, he leaves behind a reputation of
courage, congeniality, morality and genuine concern for others. His
association with us was brief but inspiring. For me, personally, it is
the loss of a dear friend. I particularly ask that if there is anything
whatsoever I can do for you or your family, that you write to me.

W. F. CONNOLLY, LT, USN
Commanding

JIM ROST IN THE BEER BARGE, YRBM 20

JIM ROST WEARING HIS FLAK OUTFIT

JIM ROST ON THE BRIDGE, USS EATON (DD510), 1967

TANGO BOAT ON PATROL, PHOTO BY JIM ROST

HELICOPTER ON TANGO BOAT, PHOTO BY JIM ROST

AIRBOATS AT VINH GIA, PHOTO BY JIM ROST

TANGO BOAT BEACHED ON VINH TE CANAL, 1969

RAG BOAT AT VINH GIA, PHOTO BY JIM ROST

TANGO BOAT ON PATROL AT DUSK, VINH TE CANAL, PHOTO BY JIM ROST

Twelve

Jimmy

When I made my first phone call to David Rost, I explained who I was—a Vietnam Navy veteran wanting to speak to a member of Jim Rost's family. There was a pause, and then he said, "I am Jimmy's brother." In all subsequent communications with David he has referred to his brother as "Jimmy". When I met with David and two of his siblings for nearly four hours at the family home in Malverne, NY, we talked about Jimmy.

He was the youngest of five in a strongly religious and Catholic family raised on Long Island. There was a gap between the older children and him. He had been a "surprise" baby, the youngest one who came along unexpectedly to round out this very nuclear family. His brothers and sisters helped raise him and, in so doing, he became the focus of their affection. They watched out for him. When he was killed in Vietnam it was like a huge door had been slammed in their faces. Jimmy wasn't coming home.

With the help of my GPS, I had found the Rost residence. Malverne is a small town typical of the suburban housing developments, like Levittown, that were built during and after World War II. The Rost two-story home had a single car garage attached to the house and was constructed of clean, well-kept white siding framed in brick. It seemed small by today's standards but, in the 1950's, had been the home of James and Dorothy Rost and their five children. It is still the home of David Rost, a lifelong bachelor who is now retired. He had invited his two sisters, Mary and Joan, to join him in talking with me about their brother. His brother Paul lives in Arizona and was unable to come.

When I rang the doorbell, David came to the door and invited me into the kitchen. "Before you sit down," he said, "I want to show you around the house. This is the place where we were all raised." We walked up the stairs to the second floor, and he opened the door to a bedroom. "This was the boys' room," he said. "I have left most everything the same as it was when Jimmy was here. You can see some of his college and Navy memorabilia still tacked on his bulletin board. These are some of the books he was reading. Over in the corner are some boxes with all of his correspondence from Vietnam." The room seemed unchanged since 1969.

After seeing the bedroom, we walked back down from the second floor of the house, and David asked me to follow him to the basement. It looked like a basement from the 1950's and '60's. Nothing much had changed. Around the circumference of the cellar was one of the old miniature HO model train tracks with the engines and cars still sitting on the rails. "Jimmy and I built this," he said. Then he pointed out some model ships sitting on tables nearby. "Jimmy really had a love of boats and ships, and he also built these. We spent a lot of time here and I decided to leave the basement pretty much the way it was when he was here."

Jim Rost had died more than forty years ago, but he was very present in this house. The memory of who he was had been frozen in time in the home where he had lived. I felt like I was walking on hallowed ground.

Jim Rost's background, like mine, was deeply rooted in the Christian faith. His mother and father had brought up their children in the Catholic Church and Jim had gone to Pius X, a Catholic preparatory seminary for young men headed toward the priesthood. I asked his siblings what had influenced him to change course. Part of it seems to have been related to his discovery of girls. "When his middle brother was married, I think his views changed," his sister Mary said. "He met a girl around that time and was quite smitten by her. That would have been 1962, the year he graduated from high school." Joan, the other sister, thinks that her brother's thinking had changed even before that: "He had indicated that he wanted to go to sea, and had been interested in going to the Naval Academy. But, because of high blood pressure, he couldn't pursue that." Whether it was girls or a love for the sea, prior to graduating from high school, Jim Rost had decided not to pursue a theological education.

Jim's good friend from high school days, who attended another Catholic school, Bill Donahue, believes that even by his junior year, Jim had decided not to pursue a seminary education. "While we discussed religion, it was not as intense or detailed as discussions I had at my high school. With a few exceptions, I do not recall much discussion of serious religious books." Bill Donahue's observations were that "his favorite reading material concerned the Navy and sea stories. I remember he was very taken with WWII books and movies, especially those which described destroyers and destroyer escorts." When I had known Jim Rost in Vietnam, I had tagged him as an "engineer" but also as someone who would discuss theological and political issues. Bill Donahue was painting a similar picture: "Actually, Jim talked mostly about science and the Navy during his high school years. He loved astronomy, built a telescope and avidly read navy and science fiction books. In contrast, he had less interest in the theological questions that religious people discuss first when the talk turns to science." As a matter of fact, Jim Rost, while in the Catholic preparatory seminary, had authored a regular article in the school newspaper on science. Many of his articles dealt with his interest in astronomy and space exploration.

Bill Donahue remembers clearly when he found out that Jim Rost had decided not to attend seminary after his graduation from the high school level preparatory school. He and Jim were working together in summer jobs at a factory on Long Island, and one day Jim announced that he had decided not to go to seminary but to take a full-time job at the factory after high school. Donahue was shocked. He knew how smart Jim Rost was and swung into action to try and steer him toward college. His parents had no idea that Jim was headed for a factory job. So, according to Bill Donahue, "I threatened to tell the highest authority (Mrs. Rost) if he didn't change his mind . . . . Our talk then turned to college, followed by a Navy career. It was the only other scenario he would consider." A good high school friend had jumped in to give good—though unsolicited—advice to Jim Rost. Jim's older brothers were engineers, and that probably also influenced his final decision. In the fall of 1962, Jim Rost did not take the factory job on Long Island; instead, he entered the Stevens Institute of Technology in Hoboken, NJ as a freshman.

When Jim Rost graduated from college, he applied and was accepted for Officer Candidate School (OCS) at Newport, Rhode Island. Following his commission as an Ensign, he chose the route of the engineer becoming Main Propulsion Assistant on DD-510, the *USS Eaton*. From the surface Navy, he would volunteer and report for duty with the Mobile Riverine Forces in Vietnam. Again, it seems, his friend Bill Donahue would help influence this later decision. For anyone who has grown up on Long Island, a great pastime has always been boating or sailing on the Great South Bay. To get out on the bay was a passion of Donahue's, and he had purchased 17-foot plywood, V-hull boat with a 75 horsepower outboard engine to pursue his dream. One day, when Jim Rost was home on leave from the Navy, Bill Donahue invited him for a trip on the boat. As you follow Bill

Donahue's description of that day out on the Great South Bay, you can see the wheels turning in Jim Rost's mind.

> *"I recall it was sunny, maybe 80 degrees, with a mild breeze. We motored about five miles through narrow channels, then into the open bay and the sand beaches beyond. When Jim took the controls, he was a changed sailor. He opened the engine to maximum speed, aimed at the largest wakes and waves, and did everything but sink it. We covered a large part of the Bay at high speeds, using most of the three, six-gallon gas tanks in a surprisingly short time. I was mentally wincing, knowing that I would have to re-caulk the boat the next week.*
>
> *Jim said he liked the powerboat experience. He had been fishing in small boats with his father, but this gave him a completely different view of boating on the Great South Bay.*
>
> *While returning to the dock, I offered to sell him the boat if he was going to return to New York. I had my eye on a new fiberglass model. He said that was not in his plans. Jim then said something that I did not understand at the time. He said I had helped him make up his mind, and he thanked me several times as we drove home. He did not explain further . . . . He did not mention the Brown Water Navy to me at that time."*

It does not take a great stretch of the imagination to see Jim Rost making up his mind on that wonderful day of boating on the Great South Bay. He was going to move from ships in the U.S. Navy to smaller craft. In the records that were sent to his family after his death is a request card filled out in Jim Rost's handwriting, requesting a new assignment from ships to boats.

It is dated August 1968. Specifically, he requested an assignment to either a fast coastal patrol boat designated as a "PB-84 Class"; or, in the alternative, he wanted to be assigned as Chief of Staff/ Operations Officer for a River Assault Division in Vietnam. The Navy honored his second request. He received orders for boat training and survival school on the West Coast. From there, he was sent to River Assault Division 132 in Vietnam. It was there, in operations along the Vietnam/Cambodian border on Vinh Te Canal, that I would meet him.

The day that I met with three of Jim Rost's siblings, we spent a lot of time talking about Vietnam and about Jim's life there. However, it was also a time for them of recounting the events surrounding his death. Jim's father had died in 1961, but his mother was alive and living in the Malverne home in 1969 when the Navy sent their "next of kin" notification contingent to tell her the bad news. "She was sitting right over there at the table," Joan said, "when she saw the Navy men in uniform coming up to the front door."

Mary continued, "She knew what it meant when she saw them. She called me right after on the telephone and said, 'Some men from the Navy came.' I knew what it meant and so came right over." In keeping with the protocol of informing next of kin, the Navy men who came stayed until Mary arrived.

In listening to this story, you can almost see it being played out in slow motion. A woman sitting in a chair, looking out her front window at a daily common scene on a Long Island street, and then, across the street a car pulls up, and slowly, two men in Navy uniforms get out of the car and begin to walk with a serious, solemn look toward her front door. They are there to tell her news that she knows is coming but doesn't want to hear. Before they even push the doorbell, she knows that everything in her life has changed. As Mary succinctly put it: "She was very bitter about it. He was her youngest, kind of like a 'surprise' baby. She felt that God had played a pretty good trick on her. She was very affectionate toward this last child. I don't think she ever got over it."

Joan also talked about the long-term effect on her mother. "She was 61 when he was killed," she said, "and 83 when she died. I don't think she ever fully recovered from it." In her later years, Mrs. Rost began to develop memory problems. As Joan put it: "Sometimes, I would ask her who her children were and she would go through the four of us and then stop and say, 'Wasn't there one more?' And, I would say, 'Yes, Jimmy, he was killed in Vietnam'. Then a look of tremendous pain would go across her face, and she would remember. A few minutes later, she would start through the whole cycle again. But, for that moment, she would remember."

The recounting of these two daughters reminded me of an adage I once heard on how casualties in war affect families: "The life of a soldier can end in a second, but the pain of the family goes on forever." The story of Jim Rost's mother was proof this was true.

Our conversation turned to what was happening in Malverne at the time of Jim's death. The movie *Born on the Fourth of July* had depicted a split community on Long Island, with people taking sides both for and against the war. Mary was very explicit about the reality of this. "When Jim was killed, many of my friends were against the war. They would keep their mouths shut around me because of my brother. But I also had ambivalent feelings . . . ." Jim, himself, apparently never voiced his own views before heading for Vietnam. "I know that his girlfriend, who was Jewish, was very anti-Vietnam," Mary said. "I think he admired her for what she believed, but I am not sure that he believed the same thing. He volunteered so he must have had his own views."

When Jim had gone home on leave before departing for Vietnam, Mary tried to discuss the issue with him. "I sat on the sofa right over there and talked with him the last time he was here. I asked him about the war. I told him that I was fearful that he would come home in a pine box."

"Did he answer you?" I asked.

"Not really," she said. "He looked at me quizzically as if to say, 'What's going on in your head?'"

A third party, a former friend of a deceased brother, is not a lot of help in situations like this, but I offered some of my own motivations for volunteering to go to Vietnam. "I think his motives for volunteering were mixed, and I know that mine were," I said. "Part of it was not being happy on the ship I was serving on. Part of it was that it was our generation's war. I didn't believe that I should try and duck it. Part of it was that, in Vietnam, you could have a command as a young officer, something that you couldn't get in the regular Navy on a big ship."

We will never know for sure why Jim Rost volunteered for the Brown Water Navy—but he did. He may have actually made the decision that day on the Great South Bay on Bill Donahue's boat when he felt the thrill, freedom and exhilaration of driving a fast boat at full speed with spray in his face under a blue sky on a balmy afternoon just a few minutes drive from the house he grew up in.

* * *

If ever there were a loyal, dedicated brother, it would be David Rost. David didn't worship his younger brother, but he held him in great respect. During his own lifetime, David Rost has kept his brother's memory alive and has been the family's point man in maintaining contact with former friends and Navy colleagues. He also wrote to Jim's classmates at Pius X and at the Stevens Institute of Technology, asking them if they had insight into what had prompted Jim to join the Navy and, in particular, to volunteer for Vietnam.

Throughout his youth, Jim Rost had shown an incredible curiosity for building and constructing things. One of David's earliest memories was of Jimmy building towers from what he described as "American Bricks", a type of toy. Later, this was followed by Jimmy helping him build a layout for the model trains that are still in the basement of the Rost home. Jim later, in high school, became enamored with the mysteries of space, so he bought the components and built his own telescope. His interests expanded to ships and he would build models of ships in the basement. He purchased books describing U.S. Navy ships going back to the beginning of the Navy. Jim also became an avid HAM radio operator and had antennas stretching across the property of his home.

This iteration of the upbringing of Jim Rost brought him alive for me again. I remember this inquisitive side of him, the willingness to talk about the unknown and what was over the next horizon. David related that while at the preparatory high school for seminary, Jim had taken up an avid interest in learning Latin. He had tacked a quote from Virgil to his bulletin board: *forsan et haec olim meminisse juvabit,* "Perhaps someday it will help to have remembered even these things!" He was quiet but had a great sense of humor.

One question I have often asked myself, would Jim Rost have stayed in the Navy had he survived the Vietnam War? There is evidence on both sides. It is clear that he had discovered girls and had dated a few and exchanged letters with some. He had probably discovered enough about himself to realize that he was not cut out for the celibate life of the priesthood. But would he have left the Navy to return to civilian life? Though some of the letters he wrote home from Vietnam showed a growing distaste for the Vietnam War, he was also supportive of President Nixon's leadership in trying to bring the war to an end. David Rost posed the same questions to himself. "He had great frustration with the Navy bureaucracy, but there is a bureaucracy in any large organization, especially the government, and the Navy is a very old part of it," he wrote describing his brother's evolving decision about whether or not to stay in the Navy. When I saw all of the model ships that had been built by Jim Rost and, after having read the account of his day of boating with Bill Donahue on the Great South Bay, I come down on the side of the Navy. Despite the bureaucracy, Jim Rost was, at heart, a naval officer and engineer. I think he would have settled down with a beautiful woman who could live a Navy life and then gone on to become an Admiral.

*　　*　　*

During the long afternoon I spent talking with the three Rost siblings, the one who spoke the least was his sister, Joan. Joan reminded me of Jim. He had been that way. We would sit in the wardroom of the YRBM-20 or in the beer barge tied up to it, and I would immediately begin my blather about the latest happenings in the Navy, politics, theology or the war—and he would just sit there and soak it up. But, finally, when he did speak, he would point at something either consistent or inconsistent with what I was saying and would give a rational explanation of his position. Intellectually, he was no pushover. There was a reason for each of his views,

In a similar, deliberate way, his sister Joan did that during our meeting in January in Malverne, NY. She thought and thought about her brother and our conversation about him and then six months later, she sent me a long, detailed letter. Some of the vignettes from that letter helped me better understand who Jim Rost was.

"Everyone in the family called him Jimmy. He was the baby of the family. He was a beautiful baby with very fair skin, blue eyes and blonde hair . . . . He was chubby and had big cheeks so he was nicknamed 'Winston Churchill'. When the rest of us went to school, he would tell my mother that 'my people are going to school', and when we returned from school, Jimmy would say 'my people are coming home'. We called him 'King James.'"

"Our father loved to go fishing—usually deep sea fishing and often at Montauk Point, way out to the east from our house. Jimmy went with him a few times but not because he liked fishing—he liked boats."

"My siblings and I have had many discussions over the past few months about when Jimmy decided not to become a priest. We feel it quite possible that he had made the decision before my father died (1961) but did not want to disappoint him and/or did not know how to tell him. My mother, who was not a Catholic and who had argued against Jimmy entering a prep seminary at the age of 13, was probably relieved that he was on a different path."

"When we found out that Jimmy had volunteered to go to Vietnam, to the canals there on a small boat, we were all shocked. My mother was extremely upset about his decision, but he probably did not know it. She most likely didn't communicate this to him. My mother had always

honored and respected our decisions even when she disagreed with them."

"At Christmas (1968), I knew that I would not see Jimmy before he left for Vietnam in May. He was going to California for training and would not come back east before going to Vietnam. When I saw him for what turned out to be the last time, I gave him a hug and said: 'Don't do anything stupid like getting shot.' He said: 'Don't worry, I won't do that'".

"I saw no justification for war but, after his death, I had to find a way to respect my brother's decision and feel OK about it. I finally decided that Jimmy made his decision to go to war with honorable intentions and he tried to live his life as he saw best. I honor him for that. I am still against wars and killing, even in self-defense. But I have never been and will never be a war protester. I cannot do that. I cannot do that to the sacrifice Jimmy and many, many others made for our country."

"Losing Jimmy of all her children was, to me, the most terrible loss possible for my mother. I don't think she ever fully recovered from it. I do not believe in 'closure', that word used by people who have no idea that the pain remains forever. People, at least most people, learn to live with pain but it is still a huge scar on your heart. For my mother, the pain made a visible change in her. It took her a long time to 'come back' and I don't think she ever enjoyed life as fully as before. Yes, there were many joyful events in her life but there was always the pain not so far beneath the surface."

"Jimmy's funeral was on December 1, 1969, two weeks to the day after he was killed. The day of the funeral was very cold. At the cemetery, it started to snow lightly. When the gun salute went off, the baby I was carrying jumped in my womb. Every time the guns went off, my soon-to-be daughter jumped in my belly."

"When I go to the Vietnam Veterans Memorial in Washington, D.C., I touch Jimmy's name and feel somehow I am still touching him. A few years ago, I had the distinct honor of reading his name at the Vietnam Veterans Memorial. As I stood on the platform, with my back to the Memorial, a plane was taking off from National Airport nearby. The noise from the plane was very loud. So I stood at the microphone and waited, waited and waited even longer until the sound of the plane had faded. Then I said proudly and with as much presence and clarity and love as I could muster, 'my brother, James Francis Rost, Junior.'"

*　　*　　*

For all of the Rost siblings, Jim Rost had always been "Jimmy". Paul Rost had been in Vietnam as an Air Force fighter pilot at about the same time his youngest brother had been on river boats in the Mekong Delta. Paul had seen plenty of action and always thought his own death more probable than that of his little brother. In reflecting on his brother's death he wrote, "It should have been me. Had I been killed while flying, I would have wanted everyone to know that at least this was what I had wanted to do since I was ten or twelve. I loved it and had no regrets." However, in Paul's view, "Jimmy was a different case. He was a gentle soul, perhaps too naïve for this war and what it entailed. I know that he felt for the Vietnamese people and the trials and tribulations they were going through just as much as our troops. That was noble. Even after all of these years, I know that we must accept that he was doing what he chose to do, but it is still hard to accept his loss."

*   *   *

A quiet descended on the room in the Rost family home. I was finally ready to leave on that January day. I was exhausted, and I think we all were, from talking about this man, and then visiting his gravesite. We were emotionally drained. David, Mary and Joan invited me to stay for food, but I felt a need to move on and get back to my motel. We stood up to say goodbye.

Mary thanked me for coming. "This time with you was very special," she said.

"He lives on with all of our memories of him," I responded. "He was a guy who stood for the right things. That's all good. It's too bad his life ended so young."

"He's eternally young," David said immediately, and then Joan spoke for all of the siblings: "We talk about how old we are and I just had my 70th birthday. But then, there's Jimmy. He is forever young."

James Francis Rost
Our Lady of Lourdes, Malverne

Sartor 3, 4   Sartor was student newspaper;
Yearbook 4   he had a science column
Intramurals 1, 2, 3, 4

**JIM FRANCIS ROST AT CONFIRMATION IN 1956
AND IN HIS ST. PIUS X YEARBOOK IN 1962**

JIM ROST'S HOME CHURCH, MALVERNE NY

JIM ROST'S BROTHER, DAVID, AND HIS SISTERS, MARY AND JOAN, AT THE ROST FAMILY HOME, MALVERNE, NY

Thirteen

R & R

Every American in the military in Vietnam looked forward to two weeks of R&R—Rest and Recuperation. Soldiers and sailors, in their usual irreverent and simple way, renamed it "I & I"—Intoxication and Intercourse. What it really was, though, was a well devised strategy by military leaders and the U.S. Government to break up your one-year tour in Vietnam with a two week leave (with pay) and a free plane ticket to a destination of your choice somewhere in the Pacific. It was on everyone's punch-list to schedule an R&R destination almost the day of arrival in-country. It broke up your military commitment into two discernible and distinct time periods—from the time you went to Vietnam until R&R and, then, the remaining time between R&R and your return to the United States. It gave you something to look forward to and made your military commitment seem shorter. While on R&R, you could return to normal life outside the war. You could relax and restore your sanity and appreciation of civilian life; then you would come back to Vietnam to finish up your tour.

As I look back on R&R, I believe that troops stationed now in places such as Afghanistan would be well served by a similar policy. Today, however, we don't have a draft, so we don't have a large enough military. Instead, we send the same troops back time and again to war zones. Currently, the numbers of professional military who actually fight wars is relatively small, and many have been rotated back and forth to the Middle East on an almost continual basis. It is no wonder that we hear of Post Traumatic Stress Syndrome or other mental problems in our military. Soldiers are human beings, not robots. They are susceptible to breaking down under the continual stress caused by exposure to combat. In the Vietnam era, R&R wasn't a panacea for avoiding all of that, but it was a practical release from the tension of living in an uncertain war-torn country.

In Vietnam, it was very unusual for a soldier, sailor or airman to have multiple tours in the country unless he or she volunteered or requested it. Most members of the military knew that if they survived their one-year tour in Vietnam, that would be it. They could then go home or be reassigned to another duty station with the understanding that they had "served their tour." Not only were normal orders of a one-year duration; that commitment was broken up by R&R. In that sense, it was a more fair system than what we see today. I have always thought that it was a policy for which the military deserved some credit. It cost Uncle Sam some money, but it also extended the useful combat life of the soldier. It was an uptick in what otherwise could be a long and very downbeat year.

There was also fairness in the way the policy was administered. Technically, you were eligible to request R&R the very day you arrived in Vietnam, though it usually wasn't granted until the last six months of your tour. The program was set up so that the highest priority was given to those who had spent the longest time in-country. Thus, if you had already spent 11 months in Vietnam, you came higher in the pecking order for R&R than the person who had just arrived or who had spent only six months in the country. Rank had nothing to do with it. The Private First Class or a Navy Seaman had as much right to R&R as a General or an Admiral. I never heard anyone criticize the military for cheating on this system. People lived by the rules and they were applied equitably.

The choice of your destination was also equitably applied. Those who had been in-country longest had a first priority on where they wanted to go. Many men, especially those married, chose Hawaii because they could join their wives and dependents there for their two weeks of R&R. That is what Bob Olson did just a few weeks before he was killed, when he flew to Honolulu to see his wife and child. Many, however, wanted to go to Australia, and there was always a long waiting list for flights there. Americans tend to be xenophobic—they want to see people like themselves, and Australia was the destination closest to looking like home that there was in the Far East. A common expression among GI's was that they hadn't seen a "round-eye girl in months!" I never interpreted that to mean that they didn't like to look at Vietnamese girls. Girls of any culture have always been on the American male radar screen. But they wanted to see women like they had known at home, and so Australia was a top destination pick for R&R. It may seem crass, but it was reality.

I recall men returning from R&R trips to Australia claiming that they had met a beautiful girl and been invited to meet her family. They framed their experience in the context that the fathers of these girls had even encouraged a relationship with their daughters. A lot of this was ascribed to Australians still loving the Yanks for defending them in World War II. According to some I talked with, Navy men were especially welcome in Australia. They claimed that Australians still talked about the Battle of the Coral Sea in 1942 when the U.S. Navy confronted and defeated a Japanese armada that was moving to invade Australia. It may have all been apocryphal, but the spin was consistent; Australians still loved Americans and Australian women especially loved American military men. It didn't really matter whether it was true or not. The queue lines in Vietnam for men lining up to go to Australia kept getting longer. I was told, though never verified it, that you had to be in-country for at least eleven months to have any chance for R&R in Australia.

In late December, 1969, I was transferred to the staff of River Patrol Flotilla Five (RIVPATFLOT 5) in Binh Thuy. My days as a patrol officer were over and I had become a part of the Navy's priority program of "Vietnamization," turning U.S. boats and Naval Base operations over to the Vietnamese. The change in assignment also provided an opportunity for R&R and, after all of the action on the Vinh Te Canal, I was ready for it. Plus, I wasn't interested in waiting until I had been "in-country" for eleven months to go to Australia. I had always had another destination in mind—Japan.

*   *   *

Prior to volunteering for Vietnam, I had been Operations Officer on a small ship home-ported in Sasebo, Japan. Some of the best advice I ever received came from my roommate at Officer Candidate School (OCS) in Newport, R.I., in 1967. As we neared graduation, we were required by the Navy to fill out a preference form as to where we wanted to serve in the fleet. Having grown up in upstate New York, I immediately thought of requesting a ship on the East Coast. That meant I would be able to periodically get back home from an East Coast port like Newport or Norfolk. When I mentioned my intentions to my roommate, he said: "Are you crazy? Here you are in a position to see the world and have the Navy pay for it and you want to stay on the East Coast. That's nuts!" I asked him what he was going to do, and he said that he was requesting a ship home-ported in Japan.

He was right, of course. I had traveled outside the country only once and really hadn't seen much of the world. So I followed his lead and asked to be assigned to a ship stationed in Japan. The

Navy came through and I received orders to report to a WWII era, steel-hulled minesweeper which had been converted into a degaussing ship. Historically, many ships in the Mine Force had been named after birds, and this ship was no exception. I had never heard of nor seen this kind of bird, but it must exist because the Navy had named this ship the *USS Surfbird* (ADG 383).

One tidbit of information known only to Navy men is that most Navy ships have electromagnetic coils running through their hulls. The purpose of these coils is to offset or decrease the ship's magnetic signature which, in turn, reduces its vulnerability to detonating a magnetic mine. This small ship to which I was assigned carried a portable degaussing range of magnetometers, which we could lay on the bottom of a harbor and then check and recalibrate the magnetic signatures of ships that passed over it. It was a strange and relatively unknown mission in the Navy, but it had one enormous benefit: our ship traveled all over the Far East to conduct these operations. During the first month I was aboard this ship, we traveled to seven different countries in the Western Pacific. Everyone on that ship also looked forward to the two or three weeks between deployments when we were able to stay in our homeport of Sasebo, Japan. The recruiting slogan I had seen on billboards in the U.S. was truthful. You could "join the Navy and see the world!"

While in Sasebo, I made some great friendships with officers and enlisted men who worked at the naval base. Sasebo is a magnificent natural harbor surrounded by mountains which, in places, run right down to the water's edge. It had been a major port for the Japanese Navy during World War II. Some of the American officers on the base had pooled their resources and rented a house on a mountainside with a beautiful view of the harbor. The Japanese called it "*Ogasahara Beso*". "*Beso*" was the word for "villa" and "*Ogasahara*" was the name of one of its former owners. Rumor had it that a Japanese Admiral had committed suicide in the house after having lost a major battle to the American Navy in the South Pacific in World War II. Because he hung himself instead of killing himself with a sword in the more noble death of *"seppuku,"* the house was supposedly haunted. For young American naval officers, this whole side-story of history just made the place more enticing. You could get into a taxi any place in Sasebo and say: *"Ogasahara Beso, Dozo!"* and the cab driver would say *"Hai, Hai* (yes, yes)" and within ten minutes you would be at the villa. We also soon found out that it was a place where young Japanese women from fine families would come to party with Americans.

One of the downsides of Navy life has always been the closeness of bar towns or "Navy towns" to U.S. Naval bases. It means that you can have a fast track to fun, but it also means that you get quickly introduced to the sleazy side of life. However, because Navy men are always coming and going on ships, these streets full of bars and bar girls are probably inevitable. The Navy town in Sasebo was appropriately called "Paradise Alley," but it was "paradise" only in the same sense that people confuse "fool's gold" with real gold. You could find pretty girls in Paradise Alley and, during holidays, when they dressed up in traditional Japanese *kimonos,* they could be spectacularly attractive. But getting to know a nice girl, someone with education and depth, was not easy. Girls from good families did not go to Paradise Alley. To show up on the arm of an American walking in that part of town was equivalent to announcing yourself as a prostitute or bar girl. However, being invited to meet American Naval Officers at *Ogasahara Beso* over wine and cheese and a catered dinner was not only okay but a welcomed invitation. It was there, in 1968, on the mountainside overlooking Sasebo harbor, at a *sakura* party celebrating the season of the Japanese cherry blossoms, that I met Masako. We dated steadily for more than a year until I returned to the United States for PBR training and redeployment to Vietnam.

*   *   *

It was early morning and a winter day in January, 1970, when the R&R plane from Vietnam landed at the Yokota Air Base outside Tokyo. I knew it was going to be a bittersweet homecoming with Masako. We had said our goodbyes nine months earlier. We both thought our romance was over. But we had also talked of getting together one more time, if I could work out a trip when I came back to the Far East, to Vietnam. I remember it being cold as I stood at the Yokota train station shivering in an overcoat. I had tried to buy warm clothing to bring from Vietnam, but it was hard to find. South Vietnam was a tropical climate and there were no wool sweaters. I knew that the first thing Masako would do when we met would be to take me to a department store and help me buy something warmer. She owned a clothing and shoe store in Sasebo and would always be sure that whatever I bought was stylish. She was way ahead of me in that department. I have never been far from my farm upbringing, and being fashionable was something I was (and still am) foreign to. When we met in Tokyo, she took me right to a clothing store for some warmer clothes and, as I remember, some Izod sweaters.

Masako was my second flame, so to speak. My first had been in college. My third would become my wife, of now forty years. I have always had fond memories of old girlfriends and, to my wife's credit, she has always accepted that. In part, she has strong, similar memories of a first marriage that didn't work out. Now that we are both of retirement age and have four children and eleven grandchildren, it doesn't seem to matter much that there were others along the road of life. I am a country-western fan and one of my favorites is Willy Nelson singing, "I'm glad they came along. I dedicate this song to all the girls I loved before." How can you not remember them? Masako had made an impact in my life. I wanted to see her again.

Although the Navy made it possible for me to see the world, that didn't mean that I would learn anything about it. Several of the men on my ship were married, and their wives and families were stationed in Sasebo. We called the married men, in jest, "brown baggers" because they were known to bring brown bags with lunch and goodies from home. I often saw these officers and their wives at the Officer's Club, and they loved being in Japan. Also, a couple of men on the ship had married Japanese women and told me that they intended to retire in Japan. There were others who created what were thought to be temporary but arranged live-in relationships. The sailors who were living with Japanese women, but not married, were called "class B brown baggers." However, most of the crew lived on the ship, and their entertainment and knowledge of Japanese women came from the bars of Paradise Alley.

I lived on the ship but also had a room in the BOQ (Bachelor Officers Quarters) on the base. Masako lived with her aging mother. I wasn't a brown bagger, either married or unmarried. I bought a small Honda sports car from a Marine who was transferred back to the States and, when our ship was in homeport, Masako and I would sometimes take weekend trips just to get out of Sasebo. She liked going to the Officer's Club located just off the naval base, but didn't want to be seen anywhere near Paradise Alley. She was concerned that someone might see us or tell her mother. Masako's father had been a soldier during the Second World War and was killed in Burma. The family had been notified of his death but never found out where he was buried. She sometimes talked of wanting to travel to Burma to try to find his remains. Her father's family had been well-to-do landowners prior to the war, but the war changed that. When the post-war American occupation took hold, large land holdings were broken up and given to individual farmers. Her mother, she said, never forgave the Americans for that. She felt that her mother would not understand her falling in love with an American. I never met her mother.

It is hard to articulate now what was going through my mind then. There was good chemistry in this relationship, but it was more than that. I taught Masako English and she taught me Japanese. In addition, she taught me what it was to be Japanese: what her culture was, what the spirit was that made up the Japanese people, their history and how they looked at life and at death. It was all totally new to me. I had never ventured far from home. My background was white, middle class, Norman Rockwell American.

Once, when our ship was in dry dock for several weeks for repairs, Masako and I took a train trip to the main Japanese island of Honshu. I saw the Ryoan-ji Rock Garden in Kyoto. Here in a crowded city was a quiet Zen garden of combed gravel interspersed with large boulders. We sat on the floor of a small gazebo and, along with others, gazed at this garden for what seemed like half an hour. No one spoke. The garden had been here for five hundred years. We went to Takarazuka and saw the Kabuki Theater. What would Americans back home think of men whose faces were painted white playing both male and female roles? This form of theater had existed for centuries in Japan. Then there was the glare and glitz of the *Ginza* in Tokyo, the new Japan with all the bells and whistles of Times Square in New York. Yet in the midst of all of this, you could walk into a small restaurant burnished with tatami mats, remove your shoes, sit around a table surrounded by paper thin walls, and be as alone and removed as if you were eating in an unpopulated forest. Americans pride themselves on their love of nature and the outdoors, but a Japanese person can sit down and look at one tree or a small stream and make that small, beautiful portrait of nature seem like the Grand Canyon. After Japan, any illusions I may have had of making quick and critical comparisons of foreign cultures with my own were swept away. Every place in the world has its own history and culture. Japan has a culture that goes back thousands of years. My own country's history, as a Western power, began just three hundred years ago when the pilgrims came to America.

One place that Masako and I liked to visit was Nagasaki. It was about an hour's drive south of Sasebo. I especially enjoyed the curving, winding coastal road that swept out of the mountains and down along the fishing towns and oyster beds of Omura Bay. My little Honda sports car, though underpowered, was slung low to the ground and could take the corners at a good speed. We would fly down hills and around bends with Masako practicing her English by saying, "Too fast!" or "Slow down!" I have never been one to avoid female admonition while driving a car. There was also a stark reminder of the Second World War on one of the mountaintops that we could see from the road. It was a high, concrete, silo-like radio tower that must have been 500 feet tall. It was from that tower that the message went out to the Japanese fleet to bomb Pearl Harbor. Here I was with a beautiful daughter of one of Nippon's warriors who had answered his country's call and been sent to his death in Burma. What a difference twenty plus years can make—the Japanese surrender in Tokyo Bay occurred in 1945. By 1968 Japan was back on its feet and becoming a world economic power, this time with American support and defended by the American Navy. I was a lucky man to be driving this Japanese car with an elegant Japanese woman down to Nagasaki where Japan's first introduction to Western culture had occurred with the Portuguese back in the sixteenth century.

Japan and America will be forever linked by another event that took place in Nagasaki, the dropping of the second atomic bomb on Japan. Masako insisted that we visit—and I had wanted to see—ground zero in Nagasaki. We stood there in silence, holding hands and looked at the huge image of Buddha with his finger pointed toward the sky, toward the heavens that rained death on this place on August 9, 1945. The most devastating of all wars ended shortly thereafter, but the memory of it will forever be engrained in the Japanese psyche. Through the winter of 1944-'45 until the war's end was announced on August 15, 1945, American airpower laid waste to this land. Much of the destruction came from fire bombs. On one windy night alone, March 9, 1945, American B-29's with napalm set fire to the wood and thatch houses of Tokyo. That one night, it is estimated that over 85,000 Japanese citizens died in the flames and a million were left homeless. Masako and I were too young to remember the war, but the Buddha wouldn't let us forget. Most American GI's who fought in the Pacific were grateful for the destruction because it ended the war. After the "fight to the death" experience in Okinawa where Japanese soldiers would not surrender and where more than 12,500 Americans were killed, President Truman became convinced that a direct invasion of the main islands of Japan could cost an additional 500,000 to 1,000,000 American casualties. In an attempt to bring the war to an end, he gave the order to drop the atomic bombs.

The bomb that fell on Nagasaki was actually meant to be dropped on a different target, Kokura. Nagasaki was a secondary target. The B-29 carrying the bomb experienced bad weather that morning and couldn't see the ground over its primary target and so diverted to Nagasaki. In one of those quirks of history, Nagasaki, the city that had been the place where Christianity and western civilization first took root in Japan, would be destroyed by an atomic bomb invented in the West.

There was another poignant moment on that particular trip to Nagasaki. Masako took me to a cottage, nestled in the woods on a hillside near the city. It was a tourist destination for Westerners and the Japanese. It was the place Puccini chose for the setting of his opera, *Madame Butterfly*—about an American Naval Officer who falls in love but never marries his Japanese sweetheart. Masako looked at me and said, "This me." Then she cried, and I cried, too. History tends to repeat itself. Another Japanese woman and another American Naval Officer would follow a similar path. Probably for cultural or religious reasons, or perhaps from just poor timing, our romance would end. I wasn't ready and she was. I was headed for Vietnam and who knew what else. Two years later, by the time I was 31, I had returned home safely from Vietnam and was ready to settle down. Jane and I fell in love and were married in 1972.

*   *   *

The last time that Masako and I saw each other was in 1970 during that week of R&R in Tokyo. For more than twenty years after that we sent each other Christmas cards. She married a Japanese, I an American. My wife says that she probably never would have married me had I not been educated and seasoned by the years I spent in the Navy. She is probably right. I had received a lot of formal education but not much practical experience in living. The Navy gave me that and took me to the Far East. I met a beautiful Japanese woman who taught me to understand another culture. But another war was going on then, and this time it wasn't against Japan. With a lot of sadness and guilt about not being able to follow through on a wonderful relationship, I said *sayonara* to Masako in Tokyo, took the train back to Yokota Air Base, got on one of those military flights filled with uniforms and headed back to Vietnam. R&R was over.

Fourteen

Transition

When I arrived back in Vietnam from R&R, I reported to my new duty station with the Navy in Binh Thuy, the headquarters for all PBR operations in the Mekong Delta. It was a welcome change from being stationed on the river itself. The base was located along the large southern branch of the Mekong River called the Bassac. Floating piers jutted out into the river, configured like a typical marina to provide mooring for PBRs and other Navy boats. The Binh Thuy facility also included an operations building, a repair facility and several barracks to house the men living there. There was an enlisted men's club and an officers' club so there was no need for a beer barge. As I recall, there was a 9 p.m. curfew that required everyone to get back to the base by nightfall; during daylight hours, men were able to travel freely down to the little town of Binh Thuy or a few miles farther to the larger city of Can Tho. There was still the threat of being attacked or mortared but, during my stay at Binh Thuy, I never remember it happening. The last major action in this area of Vietnam occurred during the Tet Offensive of 1968.

Life in Binh Thuy was a total change from life on the river. There were well-ventilated barracks and the working areas of the base were air-conditioned. At noon each day, at lunch break, men would organize a volleyball game on a self-made, sandy spot located between two of the barrack buildings. It was good exercise and, along the way, you became acquainted with nearly everyone working at the base. Vietnamese civilians also worked on the base so you didn't need to be concerned about doing your laundry or cleaning your room. When office work for the day was done, you could retreat to the O-Club (officers) or EM-Club (enlisted men), which were air-conditioned and where you could watch the evening movie. It wasn't exactly Americana, but it was much closer to a version of it than camping out on a canal bank along the Cambodian border.

The only traumatic event I recall happening at Binh Thuy occurred one day when I was driving a jeep and had slowed down in a traffic jam on the main road near the four corners of the town. A boy came over and said, "Hi, GI!" I said, "Hi!" in return, and then he twisted the watch from my wrist and took off. I exploded in anger, bounded out of the jeep, slammed the door and ran after him. He was younger, could run faster, and knew the back alleys. He dodged behind a thatched house and jumped a small canal. I jumped after him, missed, and ended up in the canal. He and my watch were now history. I scrambled up out of the canal and walked right into a nest of red ants in the middle of a banana patch. Now my mind was on the biting ants and not the watch. I headed back to the main road. The jeep was still there. I got in, started it and went on my way.

"Welcome to Vietnam," I said to myself in disgust, as I headed down the road toward Can Tho. At least we didn't have people stealing from us out on the river.

What had occasioned my departure from River Division 535 was a directive which came from the Commander Naval Forces Vietnam (COMNAVFORV), Admiral Zumwalt. He had initiated the turnover of American Navy boats and bases to the Vietnamese and, as a part of that, wanted the U.S. Navy to help make the South Vietnamese Navy more self-sufficient. Zumwalt was an up-and-comer in the Navy and knew how to deal with his superiors. Thomas Cutler, in his book, *Brown Water, Black Berets,(New York:Penguin,1988)* tells the story of how, in November 1968, Admiral Zumwalt had surprised his Army boss, General Creighton Abrams, with the news that the U.S. Navy would fully complete a turnover to the Vietnamese by June 30, 1970. At a briefing in Saigon, some of the military services were still talking about making plans to stay in Vietnam until 1976.

According to Cutler, when General Abrams heard the word "1976," he "slammed his fist down on the table so hard that an ashtray near him flipped over. 'Bullshit!' he barked. 'Don't you people realize what's happening? There is no longer a consensus for the war back in the United States. I have a letter in my pocket from the President that tells me to turn the war over to the Vietnamese.'" (Ibid.,p.303) After his outburst, General Abrams stormed out of the room. Admiral Zumwalt had heard all of this and was next on the list to brief the General. He made some changes in what he was going to say, and when General Abrams came back into the room, he promised to accelerate the Navy turnover to the Vietnamese and "projected a complete turnover of all U.S. Naval operation responsibilities by 30 June 1970 . . . When the presentation was over, General Abrams rose, put his arm around Zumwalt's shoulder and led the young vice admiral into his office." (Ibid.) Creighton Abrams now had a leader in one of the military services who was going to charge ahead on this new political and military policy for Vietnam that had come down from Washington. During 1969 and 1970, the policy of turning U.S. Naval operations over to the Vietnamese would be implemented by Admiral Zumwalt throughout his command.

The Navy, of course, had to have a new name to describe this new program. According to Cutler, "Zumwalt liked ACTOV, for 'Accelerated Turnover to the Vietnamese,' because it sounded like 'active,' and he was determined that this program was going be just that." (Ibid. p. 304) As a part of this policy, we had been training Vietnamese on PBRs since I had arrived in the country. Now, at Binh Thuy, I would be a part of creating what were called "self-help" programs, to be implemented at the new Vietnamese Naval Bases that were being established throughout the Mekong Delta.

The Zumwalt directive I read mentioned the "self-help" initiative, and that he was seeking volunteers for this new program. The message sounded as though he were looking for men who had received college degrees in agriculture back in the States. I had no formal training in agriculture but had grown up on a farm and knew how to milk cows, raise pigs, and care for chickens. Dairy cows were nonexistent in the Mekong Delta, but pig and chicken farming were staples of the economy. The Navy's goal was to introduce agriculture to the Vietnamese men who would be manning the newly established Vietnamese Naval Bases in the region. Many in the South Vietnamese Navy had grown up in cities like Saigon, and had no idea of what was involved in farming. When the deep thinkers in Saigon were notified of my background in farming, to my surprise, they sent me orders to report to Binh Thuy and become a part of the new program.

Some of my friends, when they learned what my new duties were, decided that they should give it a Navy acronym. They started calling me COMCHICKPIGPAC, "Commander Chickens and Pigs Pacific." Though it was descriptive of what I was doing, and though it was based on the great Navy tradition of naming everything with big words, the Navy brass, thankfully, never adopted it as an official name. Nevertheless, the program became a top priority for Admiral Zumwalt, and those of us involved with it were given the resources for implementing it. It also meant that, periodically, I would travel to Saigon, to the offices of COMNAVFORV, where the program was being coordinated for the entire country.

* * *

For those who served in Vietnam, there was another acronym that everyone knew: MPC (Military Payment Certificate). MPC was the American military money in Vietnam. It was technically illegal for anyone, other than an American, to own it. It was dollar-denominated paper currency and was manufactured in a size nearly equivalent to the paper currency used in a Monopoly game. You were paid in MPC, could cash checks in it at most American bases, and you could also deposit MPCs into a checking account for the purpose of making payments back home. It was illegal to use dollars (greenbacks) in Vietnam. However, MPC were as good as dollars. The Vietnamese currency was the *dong*. In truth, everyone, including the Vietnamese, preferred the MPC. The Vietnamese currency was highly inflationary, and its value varied from day to day. Though illegal, the MPC was often used by Americans in purchasing items in the Vietnamese economy, and it was also used by the Vietnamese themselves. However, in implementing the Navy self-help program, we were required to use *dong*. One of the reasons that I periodically traveled to Saigon was to receive *dong* at the official exchange rate recognized by the government of South Vietnam. I would then go to a Vietnamese vendor or to a marketplace in the Mekong Delta and use that cash to purchase pigs, chickens and the necessary feed and agricultural supplies to start small farming operations. It was a rather convoluted system but it got the job done.

The logistics of establishing a self-help farming operation were really quite simple. We would make contact with the Commander of what was, or was becoming, a South Vietnamese Naval Base. We then established a working group within our organization in Binh Thuy, and someone would travel to that location to ensure that a farming operation would work. We then trained those designated to carry it out and followed that up by scheduling a delivery of livestock. Our Commander in Binh Thuy had issued orders that gave the program a top priority on the use of transportation resources. I vividly recall one day when I needed to deliver some newborn chicks to a military base some distance from Binh Thuy. The chicks needed to be under cover and housed in a heated brooder before the end of the day, and the only way that could be accomplished was by using a helicopter. Navy operations had scheduled me for a flight at a nearby Army base. When I got to the helicopter landing pad, an Army Colonel was sitting in the passenger seat of the chopper, and he said he was sorry, but he needed the helicopter to get to Saigon. I said: "I'm sorry, too, sir, but you will have to get out. I have priority orders to get these baby chicks to My Tho and they must go now!" He couldn't believe it, but looked at my orders and saw that my priority for travel was higher than his. With a growling look I will never forget, he jumped out of the helicopter, hopped in a jeep and left. I took off with the pilot, co-pilot and 300 baby chicks and headed for my destination. This was an operation aimed at wrapping up the war in Vietnam. Not even rank was going to take precedence over that.

As a part of the "pigs and chickens" program, we established what amounted to a training center for our own staff at Binh Thuy. Not far from the base, in the City of Can Tho, was a convent and an orphanage run by the Catholic Church. A very enterprising nun by the name of Sister Anicet heard about our program and wanted to start a chicken farm at the orphanage. She saw it as a way to generate eggs to feed the children. For us, it offered the possibility of watching one of these projects develop up close. It was only a ten-minute ride by jeep to the orphanage. Sister Anicet was an amazing organizer and, within two weeks, she had this pilot project up and running. After I left Vietnam, she sent me a letter to report that the hens were laying eggs and everything had worked out.

AUTHOR WITH SISTER ANICET HOLDING THE FIRST CHICKS

SISTER ANICET WITH ORPHANS HOLDING CHICKENS

*   *   *

Not only was the United States transitioning out of the war, but men about to become Vietnam veterans were beginning to think about what they would be doing once the war was over for them. I had decided not to stay in the Navy but, other than that, had no clear direction of what I was going to do. That changed in March 1970. I received a letter from the Mayor of my hometown suggesting that I consider running for the New York State Assembly. No Democrat had won this position in 100 years, but I decided I would give it a whirl. Unfortunately, after receiving this letter, a postal strike occurred in the United States, and all mail was halted coming in and out of Vietnam. Knowing that a prompt response was critical, I decided to send a reply to the Mayor by telegram. That had its own difficulties since the only way to place a telegram was to call the Naval Communications Station at Cam Ranh Bay, a long distance from where I was and difficult to contact because of the unreliable telephone service in the Mekong Delta. Finally, one evening after midnight, when the phone traffic had subsided, I got through to the operations desk at Cam Ranh Bay. The officer who answered the phone had been a friend on Minesweepers when I was stationed in Japan. He offered to send and pay for the telegram! So, in a roundabout way, that is how I became a candidate for the New York State legislature.

(Oh, how communication has changed; my children now send messages to their friends and colleagues around the globe several times a day.)

But things then became more complex. Someone back home had decided to run against me in the primary election. A Navy lawyer friend told me that I could send a letter to voters from Vietnam as long as they were hand-addressed. Based upon that advice, I requested a three-day pass and flew to Hong Kong on an old Air Force C-47, which made weekly trips to Hong Kong from an Air Force Base located near Binh Thuy. It was a World War II era, twin-engine airplane: slow but very reliable. On the trip to Hong Kong, however, my newly launched political career almost came to an end. At dawn, as the plane touched down in the northern part of the country for refueling at Phu Bai, a mortar attack hit the base. I heard some popping going off, looked out the window of the C-47 and there, just off the runway, were some 60-millimeter mortar rounds exploding and walking their way along parallel to the plane. The pilot gunned the plane and went as fast as he could toward a taxiway. When we reached the main ramp, he yelled, "Everybody out, head for the revetments!" We all jumped out and ran, but couldn't see any bunkers or revetments for protection. By that time, the mortar attack had ceased. Since we were all hungry, we decided to go into a mess hall for breakfast. The mortar rounds had exploded close to the plane but, upon inspection, the pilot found no shrapnel damage, so, after eating, we piled back into the plane and continued our trip to Hong Kong. It passed through my mind that this was not a very good way to start a political campaign.

LTJG Rolland E. Kidder
U.S. Navy, Binh Thuy, Vietnam

RIVPATFLOT 5
FPO
San Francisco, Cal. 96627
May 25, 1970.

Dear Friend:

Recently, I declared my intention to seek the office of Assemblyman from the New York State 150th Assembly District and I am writing to request your support in the Democratic primary election on June 23rd. Due to my military obligation in Vietnam I will not be able to come home and actively campaign until July. In my absence a Citizen's Committee has been formed to represent my candidacy. However, I also wanted to contact you in this personal way to ask for your help in the election. This letter is being mailed to you under combat zone free mail privileges available to men serving in Vietnam; and I hope it will familiarize you with my background and interest in seeking this office.

Although I cannot be home for the primary, I want you to know that I am deeply committed to the campaign and to bringing better government to Chautauqua County. I consider public office to be a challenging vocation. My experience throughout college, graduate school and in the service has convinced me that we need stronger and better political leadership in America. We need men who are committed to the community and want to make it a better place to live. We need a deeper concern for the young, for the environment, for economic development, for the poor and dispossessed, for local control in decision-making. We need and deserve this kind of political leadership in the 150th Assembly District: too often in the past we have been short-changed. In asking for your support, I pledge to run an aggressive and vigorous campaign to bring better leadership to the 150th Assembly District. It is time for an infusion of new ideas and new leadership into the political life of our community.

I hope to meet you personally after my return to Chautauqua County in July. You may be acquainted with my family and the farm that my father Elliot Kidder and brother Bruce operate on S. Main St. Extension and in the Town of Busti. My brother Paul, an ex-Naval officer and now graduate student at Penn State, is managing the campaign in my absence. My background includes education in the Jamestown and Busti school systems, college in western New York, graduate school in the Chicago area, political experience working with the Democratic party in Indiana, and three years commissioned service in the U.S. Navy. During the past year I have served with the Navy as a River Patrol Boat patrol officer and as a civic action officer in the Mekong Delta. This varied background of experience has given me the kind of overall perspective which should prove valuable in political life.

I am sure you have questions about my position on state issues, my views on the war, and my platform in the coming campaign. Upon my return to civilian life and to the District, I will be able to address myself freely to these questions. In the interim, the Citizen's Committee supporting my candidacy will issue statements outlining my basic position on many of these issues. Unfortunately, my absence from the Chautauqua County area and my present involvement with the military in Vietnam, make it difficult at this time to be specific in these matters. Nevertheless, I am sure we stand together in the common concern for better and more effective government; and for more vigorous and responsive leadership in state and community affairs. If you have any questions about my candidacy and would like to write, I will be glad to respond. Again, I ask you for your support and help on primary day, June 23rd.

Sincerely,

Rolland E. Kidder

**THE AUTHOR INTRODUCES HIS CANDIDACY FOR STATE
LEGISLATURE IN THIS LETTER FROM VIETNAM, 1970**

When we reached Hong Kong, through the efforts of an old friend from college serving as a missionary there, I found a Chinese printer who could produce a letter to the folks back home asking for their political support. I placed the order and then headed back to Vietnam. The printed letters were later sent airfreight to Saigon on a commercial airline. When I went to Saigon to pick them up, some Vietnamese custom agents demanded money to release them. I balked, got angry and took a taxi to the U.S. Embassy. I walked into the Embassy in my Navy fatigues and demanded to see the Ambassador. There were all kinds of American civilian contractors sitting around waiting to get multi-million dollar contracts approved, and here I came out of the blue, a Navy LTJG, demanding to see the Ambassador! I think I created quite a stink, but it all finally worked out. The Embassy Deputy Chief of Mission quickly came to see me. I told him of the problem at Vietnamese customs and that I wasn't going to pay anyone "baksheesh," a bribe, to get these letters into Vietnam. He agreed, brought his Vietnamese secretary in, and she typed a letter in Vietnamese on U.S. Embassy stationery demanding the release of the letters. Armed with that, I returned to Vietnamese customs and showed them the letter from the Embassy. There was no further argument. They gave me the box of letters without further hassle.

Unfortunately, this episode was another lesson in the corruption problems endemic in the South Vietnamese government, but it was also a lesson in the power of the American Embassy. I had no official standing at the Embassy, but because I was in uniform and serving the country, I was ushered past all of the wannabes waiting for contracts, given priority, and my issue was dealt with. When you are an American and in the military, your country stands behind you.

From Vietnamese customs, I went to Ton San Nhut Airbase, got on a scheduled Army flight to Can Tho, and finally got the printed letters to Binh Thuy. From there, with the help of friends, I addressed the letters to the voters back home. The mail strike finally ended and the letters went out. It was an auspicious start to a campaign that would end in failure. Though I won the primary while in Vietnam, I lost the general election to the incumbent upon my return to the States. Yet the whole experience whetted my appetite for politics and, in 1974, I ran again and was elected to the New York State Assembly.

I was not an anti-war advocate when I came home from Vietnam, but I have never held it against men who came home and then became involved in the anti-war movement. It was certainly their right to do so, and by 1970 the country had turned against the war. I can't say, though, that I came home and was a defender of the Vietnam War either. I just didn't talk much about it. From my vantage point, the war was already winding down, and I didn't think that more anti-war rhetoric would shut it down any sooner. Men were still dying there, and I knew several who had died. More would continue to die before the war would end.

I thought of Tozer, Olson, and Rost. Somehow, in their memory and out of respect for them, it didn't seem appropriate to jump into the political debate. I believed that most who had gone to serve their country in Vietnam were well intentioned. Many didn't want to go, but they responded to call of their country and went. It may have been a war of choice at the political level in Washington, but it was not a choice for many people serving in the military. It was their civic obligation and they responded. Many knew that the outcome might not be good, but they went anyway. It was our generation's war.

*   *   *

Another positive aspect to working in Binh Thuy was the opportunity it gave me to meet more Vietnamese. Vietnamese civilians worked on the base and, with my job in the self-help program, I was meeting many in the local community who were involved in agriculture. During my days on the river as a Patrol Officer, I saw Vietnamese civilians every day, but at a distance. In my new job, I was meeting them and talking with them on a regular basis. To help me interface with the Vietnamese, the Commanding Officer of River Patrol Flotilla Five, Captain Faulk, assigned his Vietnamese secretary to assist. She was tall and pretty and her name was Co Hua. She spoke good English and was an excellent typist. She became my interpreter when dealing with the South Vietnamese Navy and in working with people in the local Vietnamese economy.

While patrolling on the river, sailors made the general distinction between women as being either young and pretty (a "Co"), or older and not so pretty (a "Ba"). In describing the occupants of a sampan, for example, you could hear an American on the radio say something like: "We've pulled over a sampan with a couple of Ba's and a Co, one kid and an old Papasan. We've checked their ID and everything is OK." A Vietnamese person wouldn't have known what was being said—it was Americanized Pidgin English. In the Vietnamese language, *Co* actually meant "Miss," and *Ba* was the word for "Mrs," so Co Hua, was an unmarried young woman. She was also as straight as they come. There were Navy men everywhere at Binh Thuy, and you couldn't help noticing Co Hua. However, she wasn't interested in romantic attachments and made that clear to everyone. I've often wondered what happened to civilians like her who worked for the Americans during the war. People who had served in the South Vietnamese military were sent to re-education camps, essentially prisons, after the war. I hope that the same fate did not befall Co Hua and the hundreds of others like her who worked as civilians for the Americans. When I think of them, I wonder what will become of the thousands of civilians who have befriended Americans in places like Iraq and Afghanistan. What will happen to them after the Americans leave? Their fate is a part of the collateral damage from war that is often overlooked.

I was fortunate on my tour in Vietnam to have had the opportunity to be introduced to Vietnamese culture. People like Thu Trung Van and Co Hua put a human face on the country. It is a beautiful country with an interesting history. Its people are essentially the same as people everywhere: most of them want a life where they can raise a family, provide their children an education and live in peace. They are entrepreneurial and willing to work hard to better themselves. The Vietnamese also have a trait that is less common in my own country; most are patient and not looking for quick or easy answers. They understand that change takes time. When entertaining, they take the time to get to know their guests. They realize that you don't get to know others by eating a quick meal in a fast-food restaurant. Rather, you need to sit down, eat, drink, talk—and then talk some more. A family meal or a meal with friends might take several hours but, by the end, you are immersed in new friendships and feel a part of what it means to be Vietnamese.

It was no surprise, then, that the last entry made in my journal, 22 February 1970, described one of these long and involved meals. It was organized by Co Hua, included some of her friends, and was attended by Americans and Vietnamese who were working together on the Navy self-help program.

> *"This had to have been one of the most unusual and enjoyable days of my tour in Vietnam. About twelve of us—half Vietnamese and half U.S.—from 1200 to 2000 went on a picnic along the Basaac River. It was great watching the day go by. A U.S. Army truck at the place got stuck for awhile in the river, but finally got out. We spent the day cooking shrimp and beef over a charcoal pit. Stayed busy with volleyball, swimming, talking, riding water buffalo,*

> *eating more food, watching the sun go down, fixing*
> *a flat on the jeep. A real treat!"*

It also didn't hurt that the Vietnamese knew how to make terrific beer. It carried the name "33." That was one number that every American GI knew. The number for thirty three in Vietnamese was "*ba moui ba.*" Over the course of that day, we drank our share of *ba moui ba*, but we did it Vietnamese style—slowly and interspersed with a lot of water and food. Everyone had a good time. No one got drunk.

*   *   *

As my tour in Vietnam neared its end, most of our efforts at Binh Thuy continued to be focused on handing over American Navy operations to the Vietnamese. As I had come to know Thu Trung Van while training him as a Patrol Officer on PBRs, I now became introduced to other Vietnamese officers who would be taking over our Navy operations in the Mekong Delta as the United States exited the war. After work and dinner, these men often joined us for a drink in the Officer's Club and sometimes stayed to watch the evening movie. As any Navy veteran can attest, the daily ritual of watching an evening movie around 8 p.m. takes place whether you are on board a ship at sea or stationed at a base in a remote area of a foreign country. The film scheduled for one particular night at Binh Thuy was *The Green Berets* starring John Wayne. We were about halfway into the movie when I heard the Vietnamese officers begin to talk among themselves and then start to laugh. I asked them what it was all about. "There are no Vietnamese in film!" they said. "There are Chinese, Japanese, Koreans and Filipinos, but we have not seen any Vietnamese!" They laughed again. Here I was in Vietnam, watching an American movie about the war, and there were no Vietnamese in it.

The experience of watching that film, I suppose, typified the situation of most Americans. Many of us had traveled extensively throughout the Far East as a part of the Seventh Fleet, yet we couldn't tell the difference between a Vietnamese, a Korean or a Japanese. The people who lived in those countries, however, knew the difference! It was a reminder again of how far out of our element Americans were in our crusade in Vietnam. Like most Americans, I looked to Hollywood to simplify and clarify ambiguities. I was glad that John Wayne engineered a victory in that movie. He had won every battle and war he had ever played in, whether it was in World War II or the Indian wars. Maybe there was still hope for Vietnam.

*   *   *

The ultimate transition for most Americans came at the end of our one-year tour in Vietnam. It was called going home. By June 1970, Admiral Zumwalt's turnover of American boats to the Vietnamese was nearing completion. In response, the Navy came out with a directive that those of us finishing our tours would be given a two-week "early out," i.e., we could go home two weeks early. We awaited our orders and, sure enough, they came. I am not sure how many acronyms the military ever came up with, but there was one everyone serving in Vietnam knew: your orders to CONUS (The Continental United States!).

Today, a year doesn't seem that long. Christmas runs into Christmas, and birthdays seem to come and go with the snap of a finger. But in 1969 and 1970, in Vietnam, a year seemed like an awfully long time. Partly, it was the weather—it never seemed to change. It was always hot and humid, even in the wintertime. For someone raised in upstate New York, winter meant snow. In Vietnam it meant less rain but continual heat. A part of the long year also dealt with adapting to a life you had never known before. In your head, you knew that combat and the war were just anomalies, that it was all based on a failure of policy at some level. You were involved with something akin to the little Dutch boy you had read about as a kid who tried to stop the flood by putting his finger in the dike. You were a part of something that you couldn't control, but it had a beginning and, for you, would end after a one-year tour. The world of Vietnam was like experiencing a unique lifetime squashed into twelve months. There was always the trepidation of the great unknown— would your number be next? There was also the sense that, despite the vagaries of war, you were part of something big, at least big for your country and for the Vietnamese. There was something unsettling about leaving Vietnam. For Americans, it was a transition toward something better. We were going home to a normal life in a stable, peaceful world. But what were the Vietnamese transitioning to? We wouldn't find out until 1975.

Fifteen

Endgame

The last time I saw Thu Trung Van had been in 1970 when he took me on a memorable motorbike ride from My Tho to Saigon to have dinner with his family. After I left Vietnam, he held various positions in the South Vietnamese Navy. Following a fierce battle in a counter offensive against the North Vietnamese in the summer of 1972, he was promoted to Lieutenant Commander in the South Vietnamese Navy and became Commanding Officer of a PBR River Division. He had seen a lot of combat and believed that, at least in the Mekong Delta, his country was holding its own against the Viet Cong and North Vietnamese. In 1974, following the signing of the Paris Peace Accords, and after all American combat troops had been withdrawn from the country, he also became aware that the U.S. Congress had substantially reduced its funding for the Vietnam War. The impact of this was to reduce the fighting capability of the South Vietnamese. In the Vietnamese Navy it meant less ammunition, less fuel and shortages of maintenance supplies—less of everything needed to carry on the fight. Yet he and his fellow countrymen fought on under the belief that they were gradually winning the war. Their military leaders assured them that this was the case.

So it was a shock when, on the evening of April 29, 1975, Thu was called to an emergency meeting at the Naval base in Dong Tam, seven kilometers from My Tho. There he was told of a message just received from Saigon announcing that in a few hours his country would be surrendering to the North Vietnamese. Thu and his fellow Navy men were stunned. They knew that the South Vietnamese Army had been engaged in some tough battles, but they had no idea that North Vietnamese forces were sweeping south and nearly at the gates of Saigon. They were totally unprepared for this news. Now, in a matter of hours, the cause for which Thu had been fighting since 1964 would end.

Thu's Commanding Officer also announced that, in his view, those who had fought against the North could not expect good treatment at the hands of the enemy. He believed that the treatment of officers would be especially harsh. In light of the devastating news from Saigon, he had ordered that all Naval river craft at the Dong Tam Navy Base prepare to leave and join the South Vietnamese Fleet, which was gathering near Poulo Condor Island (often referred to by Americans as Con Son Island) in the South China Sea. In a matter of hours, boats loaded with food and water would be leaving to head for the open ocean. Once at sea, they would attempt to rendezvous with one of the larger ships of the South Vietnamese Navy, which, it was hoped, could take them to the nearest U.S. Naval Base located in the Philippines. Everyone at that meeting had a life-changing decision to make: would they stay in their own country, or would they leave and try to make a new life somewhere else? In Thu's case, he wouldn't have to make the decision alone. His wife and children had come from Saigon to live with him in Dong Tam. He left the meeting immediately and headed home to talk things over with his wife, Tuyet. It would be a family decision.

Can you imagine struggling with such an immense issue in such a short amount of time? America is a country of pioneers and immigrants. My own family history goes back to England and to Sweden. Virtually all of us came from somewhere else. However, I always assumed that my ancestors had, at least, some time to consider pulling up their roots and leaving for a new land. Hunger, religious intolerance, the lack of economic opportunity and the hope for a better life—these issues piled up over years. But that one night in Vietnam, with little time to deliberate, Thu Trung Van and his family had to decide whether to stay or leave the country.

As Thu headed home that night, he also reflected on the fact that there were two other members of his family to consider in this decision: his sister, Huong, and his sister-in-law, Lien, visiting for the weekend from Saigon. They had been scheduled to return to Saigon the previous day, but the road to the capitol had been blocked by fighting in Tan An. Lien was visiting friends in My Tho, and there was no way for Thu to contact her with the news from the Naval base. Huong was at home with Thu's family and, though just nineteen, she would have to decide: Should she stay in Vietnam, return to Saigon and live with her parents, or should she leave with her brother on a boat, head for the South China Sea and, hopefully, find a way to start a new life in a foreign land? There was no way she could consult with her family in Saigon. They didn't have a phone. There was no time for letters.

On his way home from the emergency meeting, Thu mulled all these things over in his own mind, including the fact that he had not been an inactive bystander in the war. He had fought for what he thought was right. He had fought for the hope of a democratic Vietnam. He had led troops against aggressors from the North. Yet he also believed what his Commanding Officer had said: things would not go well for the losing side. He framed and reframed the arguments for and against leaving the country. When he arrived home, he told his wife the bad news and explained their options. Tuyet agreed with Thu's analysis of the situation. Through tears, they began to pack suitcases. They woke up their one and three-year old daughters. Huong was told the situation. Not knowing what the future would hold, she decided to leave with them. Thu got his family and his sister to the dock back at the base by midnight. Shortly thereafter, a small armada of South Vietnamese Navy boats moved downstream on the mighty Mekong River heading for the South China Sea and to a ship they hoped would take them to a new life. Later that day, on April 30th, the South Vietnamese formally surrendered to the North. The Vietnam War was over. For Thu and his family, what their future would be was still an open question.

* * *

As I recall, I was less surprised than Thu about the fall of the South Vietnamese government. The predictions made by Bernard Fall and others seemed to have come true. My own experience in seeing just the edges of some of the governmental corruption had tainted my views. When I left Vietnam, I had an empty feeling about its future. The only possible positive resolution I saw was the eventuality, though improbable, that the North would ultimately just give up the fight as too costly. The more than decade-old war by America that was premised upon building a viable, sustainable, democratic government in South Vietnam hadn't materialized. Some in the country had benefited from the billions of dollars spent by the United States in the conflict; however, the life of the average peasant farmer was probably worse off. The burden of war tends to trickle down to the man on the street. If his lot does not improve, then any war aims tied to it are jeopardized.

Still, I was saddened by the media image at the end showing the helicopter on the roof of the U.S. Embassy, with people groping to reach it, as the last American presence left the country. I was also worried about the fallout from the War. What would become of those who had fought with us? What was their future? I was particularly concerned about the Vietnamese friend I knew best. What was going to happen to Thu Trung Van?

The answer came in a phone call in early June. My wife picked up the phone and then handed it to me. "It's from a religious organization and about Vietnam. I think it's for you," she said. When I got on the line, the caller introduced himself as being from Church World Service, an interdenominational religious organization. I knew about the organization and their work as an international aid agency. The person speaking said that he was calling from the Indian Town Gap Army Base in Pennsylvania that now served as a refugee center for people who had escaped from Vietnam.

Then he said, "Do you know a Thu Trung Van?"

That was the first I learned that Thu had escaped from Vietnam. The aid worker told me that Thu would like to speak with me, but since there were only a limited number of telephones at the base, we scheduled a time for him to call the next day.

When Thu called, he was his usual calm, cool self. He explained briefly what had happened to him and his family. Their boat from My Tho, after fighting heavy weather off the coast of Vietnam, had reconnoitered with a South Vietnamese destroyer. Three or four thousand refugees climbed aboard and were jammed on its decks. After a three-day delay, the U.S. Seventh Fleet finally granted permission for the Vietnamese ships carrying refugees to transit to the U.S. Naval Base at Subic Bay in the Philippines. When they arrived at Subic Bay, however, the Philippine government would not let them go into port flying the South Vietnamese flag. Following a day of negotiation, the vessels hoisted American flags and were then permitted to enter Subic Bay Harbor as designated ships of the U.S. Seventh Fleet.

From Subic Bay, Thu and his family, along with other refugees, were packed aboard a U.S. Navy oiler and transported to Guam. Four camps had been established in the United States to receive the refugees.

"I didn't have your address but remembered that you lived in New York State," Thu told me. "You were the American I felt closest to during the War, so I requested the East Coast." Indian Town Gap had been designated an East Coast port of entry for Vietnamese refugees, so Thu and his family ended up there. The aid workers at Church World Service at the camp were finally able to track down my phone number, and now Thu and I were back in touch.

The aid worker who called explained the situation of the refugees. "They need to have a sponsor in order to be released from this camp," he said. "Also, they cannot be released unless they have assurance of a job. We are not allowed to transfer them unless one of them has employment. We don't want them to become a burden on public assistance." Based upon this understanding, our church agreed to be the official sponsor for Thu and his family. A friend at the local hospital said that he could get Thu a night janitor job. Based on that, I scheduled a long weekend, around the 4th of July, to drive to Indian Town Gap, pick up Thu and bring him to our hometown to meet his new sponsor and employer.

The way we actually met was quite remarkable. In 1975, I was a freshman member of the New York State Assembly. It was a very busy year for the legislature: New York City was bankrupt, the State was struggling with financial red ink, and several state agencies were on the verge of insolvency. The legislature was constantly in session dealing with the problems. Fortunately, the State at the time had a strong Governor, Hugh Carey, a former Congressman from Brooklyn who was elected Governor for the first time in 1974. He was determined that the City and State not default on their obligations. The politics of the Assembly had also changed in 1974. With my election and that of another handful of upstate Assemblymen, the New York State Assembly had been organized with a Democratic majority after having had been controlled for many years by Republicans. A corollary of being in the majority is that you have the burden of governing, and there were very few Republican votes in the Assembly in 1975 for anything dealing with New York City. That meant, in the parlance of Albany politics, that freshmen Democrats like myself were always going "in the tank" to pass needed legislation.

On the week I was scheduled to meet Thu, I drove to Albany for the legislative session. My intention was to leave Albany on Thursday afternoon, drive to Indian Town Gap in Pennsylvania, pick up Thu and take him to what would be his new home. However, the Speaker of the Assembly, Stanley Steingut, interrupted those plans by calling a special session for Friday dealing again with the New York City crisis. I went into his office and explained that I would not be at the session because I had scheduled myself to finally meet my Vietnamese friend. By now, Thu and his family had been in the refugee center for almost a month. But the Speaker was concerned about my pending absence. "This will be a tough vote," he said, "and we need you here." With that statement, he picked up his phone and pushed the direct line connecting him with the Governor. He explained my situation to Governor Carey and the Governor acted. Governor Carey was a distinguished veteran of World War II, and didn't need any explanations about why, as a Vietnam veteran, my trip to meet Thu was a priority.

"You tell Rolly," Governor Carey instructed the Speaker, "to be at the Albany airport at 6 a.m. tomorrow. The state plane should be able to get him to Harrisburg around 7 a.m. It isn't far from there to Indian Town Gap. He can rent a car, bring this friend back to the airport and then fly here to Albany. All of this can be done, and he can get back here for the Special Session."

It all worked just as the Governor said, though I think Thu was quite amazed at what happened that day. He had been on boats, ships and refugee camps for the past several weeks. We hadn't seen each other in five years. We met with a warm embrace at the Indian Town Gap refugee center, and he got in the rental car. We headed back to the Harrisburg Airport and climbed into the state plane. Here he was, new to the United States, flying in a twin-engine plane to the Capitol of New York State. I explained to him the change in plans, and why I had come by plane instead of driving my car. When we got to Albany, we drove down to the Capitol and went directly to the Assembly. Unknown to me, at the last minute, the Speaker decided to cancel the session. He had been up all night negotiating legislation but, for some reason, was unable to get it done. The legislature had adjourned for the weekend. I went into the Speaker's office to thank him for helping me link up with Thu. The Speaker wasn't there, but his wife, Maddie, was sitting in the office talking to Abe Beam, the Mayor of New York City. They invited Thu and me to have lunch with them. We went out into the beautiful, ornate, and now empty Assembly chamber to eat our sandwiches. Thu looked around in awe at the setting. What an introduction to America—from refugee to having lunch in one of the oldest legislative chambers in the country with the wife of the Speaker and the Mayor of the City of New York!

Thu probably thought I was one of the most well connected politicians in the country, but it was all happenstance. He was sitting here because I had been scheduled for a special session of the Assembly which, at the last minute, was canceled. Nevertheless, it was an unforgettable moment. I would spend eight years in the Assembly, yet one of my best memories was welcoming Thu Trung Van to his new homeland, sitting and having lunch with him in the New York State Assembly chamber conversing with the wife of the Speaker and with the Mayor of one of the world's great cities.

Two weeks later, Thu and his family moved to my hometown. He had been a college graduate in Vietnam but left so quickly that he didn't have the paperwork to prove it; therefore, he had to start over. He enrolled at our community college and in two years earned his Associate Degree. Living in the snow belt of upstate New York was a totally new experience, and he and his family soon yearned for warmer weather. So, after completing community college, he moved south to Jacksonville, Florida, to finish college and receive his Bachelor's Degree. From there, he accepted a position as a purchasing assistant with Shell Oil in Houston. He retired after 25 years of service and now lives in Dallas, Texas. As with most Vietnamese refugees, he worked hard to start a new life in America. Though he still has family living in Vietnam, he is now an American citizen. His decision, made in a few hours in 1975, worked out. For others, the path to freedom outside the country was more arduous.

*　　*　　*

One of Thu's good friends, Ninh, also an officer in the South Vietnamese Navy, had a more difficult time. He, too, left Dong Tam on that fateful night and headed by boat for the South China Sea. However, when it came time to board the destroyer en route to the Philippines, he balked. He decided that he couldn't leave the country. His wife and children were not at the Dong Tam Naval Base when he received word that the country was surrendering to the North; they were living in Saigon. Ninh couldn't bring himself to leave the country without them, so he drove one of the escape boats back to Dong Tam. He then went to Saigon to see his family where he was soon arrested by the North Vietnamese for being a traitor. He was told to pack enough food and clothing for a three-day training exercise. Then he was sent to "re-education" camp for six years. These "camps" were essentially prisons to punish those who had been on what the North deemed to be the wrong side during the war. Ninh was sent to several camps, most located in jungles far from the cities. The last camp in which he was incarcerated was located near the Chinese border in the northern part of the country. After six years, he was released. He returned to Saigon. However, once out of prison, he found it impossible to get a job. Those who had served in the South Vietnamese military, especially officers, were essentially black-balled. Thu's brother had experienced a fate similar to Ninh. Though a college graduate, after six years in prison, his only choice was to work as a motorbike mechanic for the rest of his life.

After Ninh's release from prison, realizing that there was no future for him in Vietnam, he decided to try to escape from the country. Because he had been a Naval officer and trained in navigation, he was recruited to pilot a boat full of refugees to attempt an escape. He was successful and eventually reached Malaysia, where he and the others in his boat were placed in a refugee camp. From there, he received permission to emigrate to Australia. Once in Australia, as Thu had done in America, he went back to college. He finally went into business. After living in Australia for six years, Ninh was granted Australian citizenship. Once that happened, he was able to bring his family to Australia from Vietnam. In retrospect, Ninh would have been better off to leave Vietnam in 1975. He probably would have been able to reunite sooner with his family. Instead, it took him twelve years—six years in prison followed by six years in Australia—before his family would be reunited. It seems that one of the verities of war is that families get split up. The location of war can change, but there is often a common outcome, especially if you are on the losing side: you may or may not see your family again.

*   *   *

Today, the government of Vietnam remains much the same as it was after the surrender of the South in 1975—it is a one-party, communist state dominated by the North. The economy of the country has improved, but its form of governance remains unchanged. Vietnam operates in much the same manner as the government of China—from the top down. However, today, the Vietnam government's attitude toward former combatants like Thu and Ninh has totally changed. It is very pragmatic. As explained by Thu: "We are called the *Viet Kieu,* 'overseas Vietnamese.' Those of us who were former refugees number some four million. We are all now citizens of other countries, but we still support our families living in Vietnam. Combined, we send about eight billion dollars a year into the Vietnamese economy. We may have once been the enemy, but now, when we request a visa to visit the country, they welcome us. We are the beloved people!" Time may not heal all wounds, but it can change things. Today the *Viet Kieu* are welcomed back to Vietnam. They are especially welcome if they bring their wallets.

Sixteen

Vietnam Today

In describing the *Viet Kieu,* Thu was pointing to the cultural center of Vietnam that has remained since the war—the importance of the family. Americans pride themselves in ties to the family, but nothing can quite equal the role that it plays in Vietnamese culture. As Americans, we try to get home two or three times a year, usually around Christmas, Thanksgiving or Independence Day. In Vietnam, the whole country essentially shuts down for a two-week annual family celebration called "Tet." Held at the time of the Chinese New Year, it usually is celebrated in January or February. When Thu and I discussed going back to Vietnam, he specifically excluded Tet.

"You don't want to come during Tet," he said. "You will have difficulty finding a hotel or even a restaurant to serve you. Everyone goes home. The country comes to halt. It is even hard to find a taxi." We settled on an arrival of early January, three or four weeks prior to Tet.

You start to sense the change that has come over the country since the Vietnam War even before you arrive. I flew to Vietnam from Japan on China Airlines. I was seated in a row with two Americans who were interested in my reasons for going back to the country. They were younger and had only heard or read about the Vietnam War. I asked the one next to me why he was on the flight. "We're from High Point, North Carolina," he explained, "and are in the furniture business. We have three plants over here and come over to check on things every six months or so." That piqued my interest because my hometown in upstate New York had once been the capitol of the hardwood furniture business in America before it moved south to High Point. Now, apparently, High Point had lost out to the Vietnamese. What comes around goes around. The fellow from High Point talked about the low cost of labor and efficiency of production in Vietnam. He also said that that there was a strong work ethic in the country and that, though not up to American standards, the quality of the furniture was quite good. As we got off the plane and headed for baggage claim, the two Americans stayed close to me. I think that they wanted to be sure that the old, gray-haired veteran didn't have a re-entry problem.

As we were picking up our luggage, Thu came through the crowd. We smiled at one another.

When the Americans saw that I was in good hands, they said goodbye and headed for their furniture factories. I greeted Thu for what I knew would be an eye-opening visit to the country I left forty years ago.

The airport we flew into is now named Ton Son Nhat International. It is the same airport that was called Ton Son Nhut Air Base during the war. (As I understand it, the airfield was originally built by the French near a village called Ton Son Nhat, which is where its current name originates.) The terminal building for the airport looks like many airports today in the United States: endless glass-enclosed, air-conditioned corridors facing a tarmac with jetways connecting the gates to the airplanes. There were two features at the airport that reminded me of the Vietnam War: still situated on the airfield were some of the old revetments, which look like Quonset huts, and behind a cement block wall in the terminal building were some old restrooms announcing that the Americans had been here. The urinals were forty years old but still prominently displayed the name "American Standard." There was one other symbolic reminder that it was the same place I had flown in to and out of years ago. Though this was the airport for Ho Chi Minh City, the three-letter designator for the airport was still SGN. It was not only imprinted on the luggage tags; it was still the name primarily used by the Vietnamese in describing the city. If you asked someone on the street where they live, they did not say, "Ho Chi Minh City." They said, "Saigon."

For GIs who spent any time in Saigon during the War, the easiest way to describe the city today would be to say, "Take the crowded streets you remember from back then and multiply it by ten." The number of people, the number of motorbikes, the number of cars and taxis—everything seems to be ten times greater. The city has also spread out. There is now a super-highway and high-span bridge that crosses the Saigon River as you drive in from the airport, and the urban expanse of the city reaches to the borders of the airport and beyond. Downtown, you can still see places like the Continental and REX Hotels, but they are shrouded by dozens of other higher and larger hotels and new office buildings. Tu Do Street is unrecognizable. The bars and nightclubs are gone. They have been replaced by fancy department stores selling Gucci bags and designer clothes. On the Saigon River waterfront, tour boats remind you of New Orleans. Every night, loaded with tourists and with dining tables on multiple decks, these boats take a cruise up the river with the city lights as a backdrop. We took the trip and it was magnificent. Thu reminded me that the boat cruise lines are owned by the government. Nevertheless, I sensed a certain pride coming from Thu, this former Vietnamese citizen, in the obvious growth and prosperity of the homeland of his youth.

When Americans visit Vietnam today, most of them come on organized tours, stay in plush hotels and pay American prices. However, when traveling with someone who speaks Vietnamese and knows the culture, prices quickly come down. With Thu's assistance, I checked into a nice, mid-price hotel for $30 per night. We rented a car with a driver for about $60 a day. One night, in Long Xuyen, we went to local restaurant and our total bill, including drinks, was $7 per person. These are the kind of prices I remember from forty years ago. It's no wonder that people in the furniture business in North Carolina are willing to travel eighteen hours in an airplane to get here!

A good friend, Gordon, from the U.K., who had helped plan this trip, joined Thu and me in Saigon. Gordon and I decided to divide our trip into two distinct parts. We would spend a week with Thu in South Vietnam and retrace much of our journey up the rivers and waterways I had been on during the war. In our second week, we would leave Thu and the South behind and travel by air to Danang. From there, we would drive to Hue, and, on our final leg, fly to Hanoi. During the second half of our trip, we would become typical tourists and visit some of the more prominent tourist destinations in the country. We planned to end our trip in North Vietnam, where I had never been.

As a part of my preparation for the trip, I found out an interesting fact: the United States Geologic Survey had declassified the topographic maps that we had used during the war. This meant that I could track, based upon grid co-ordinates I had recorded in my Journal, the location of where we had operated on the Mang Thit River and the Vinh Te Canal. Combined with road maps now available on Vietnam, we would be able to drive to some of these locations. Thu assured us that the driver he had hired would have no problem getting us there.

The day after our arrival, we left Saigon in our SUV rental car and turned onto Highway #1-A, which, during the war, was called Highway #1. The road goes south from Saigon to My Tho, then turns west toward Vinh Long. The highway is still packed with traffic, though now there are no military vehicles. It is no longer the two-lane clogged artery that it once was. It is a four-lane road and, in some areas, is divided by a median. The forty miles to My Tho were lined with industrial parks, one after the other. Trucks, carrying goods and produce to and from these areas and from farther away in the Mekong Delta, constituted a continual stream of traffic. The trucks were interspersed with buses transporting tourists to and from the organized Mekong Delta tour of waterways and floating markets. Added to this were hundreds of motorbikes, still the preferred means of travel in the country.

There was one new aspect to the landscape that I hadn't seen in 1969: the presence of an electric power grid. Power lines were everywhere. There was electricity in the villages along the Mang Thit River. There were power lines running the length of Vinh Te Canal. Tall steel trellises supporting high tension lines which connect the grid were visible from the road. It is clear that the electrification of Vietnam has been an important part of its economic resurgence. With electric power, you can now process food or manufacture a product virtually anywhere in the country.

At My Tho the highway turned west and, after another forty miles, reached the Mekong River. Another surprise was waiting for us: a suspension bridge spanning the river, which seemed as huge as the Golden Gate. PBR sailors would have a hard time imagining this. Where there were once ferries plying back and forth with long lines of traffic backed up, now you go through a toll booth, speed up a ramp onto a four or six-lane bridge deck, and in a few minutes you are over the river. There is a similar bridge over the Bassac River near Can Tho. There are still barges moving heavy loads of aggregate and fuel on the river, but most commercial traffic and time-sensitive agricultural production now travel by truck. The big rivers in the Mekong Delta are no longer a barrier which need to be circumvented with a helicopter or airplane, or require a long wait and delay for a ferry. Now you drive over them.

After crossing the Co Chien branch of the Mekong River, we turned left and followed the signs to Vinh Long. It was time to eat, and we stopped at a restaurant on the water's edge. Large sampans with canvas tops were pulled alongside; British and Australian tourists were disembarking for lunch. Vinh Long was the end of their Mekong Delta Tour, and buses were parked nearby to take them back to Saigon. We headed east and downstream from Vinh Long, coming finally to the type of old road system I remembered. It was one, or sometimes two lanes wide with water-filled potholes. We slowed down to 20 miles per hour to save on the shocks and bounced along, heading toward the Mang Thit River. We drove past a myriad of terra cotta and brick kiln factories situated along the road. Finally, the road ended. The Mang Thit River was directly ahead, and a small motorized ferry was crossing to the Village of Quoi An. It seemed as though nothing much had changed here. This could have been a scene from 1969.

Thu went to the water's edge and engaged in conversation with a young sampan driver. Soon, for a $25 rental, we headed south on the Mang Thit. I had brought with me a photo from 1969 of an old French church and, in a couple of miles, it came into view. The driver beached the sampan in front of the church, and we clawed our way up the bank. The church no longer has a steeple, but the main sanctuary of the building is the same. It had been partially destroyed and abandoned when I was here the last time. Today, it is again in use and has an active congregation.

Thu interpreted for us as we introduced ourselves to a family living next door to the church. The house was small, built of brick with a tile roof. It had electricity, and a ceiling fan was moving in the kitchen. A Honda motorbike was parked outside. An elder son in his 20s, with a cell phone snapped to his belt, talked with us. He and his family have lived here for only five or six years. An older neighbor who was around during the war came by and joined in the conversation. We talked about the war and that I had been here.

We didn't mention that this was the location where Captain Bob Olson killed a Viet Cong guerilla with a pop-flare.

The young son with the cell phone typified this new country. There are now more than 90 million people living in Vietnam, and more than half of them are under the age of 35. They have no memory of the war.

We climbed back into the sampan and headed to the village of Quoi An. From what I could see, the old Army MATS compound at Quoi An had been converted into what looked like a town hall. Some of the old concrete we had poured to lift the village marketplace from the mud was still there, but now the entire market was paved. The small market pavilion that was there during the war had been replaced by a much bigger building and, again, we noticed that every home in the village had electricity. There were also cable lines strung between houses carrying television and Internet services. This was a far cry from the Quoi An I witnessed in 1969 when there was only one television set and no one believed that Americans were landing on the moon. I had some old photos of the village that I began to show to a few people.

Soon a crowd surrounded me.

"That's my grandmother!" someone called out.

"There are my aunt and uncle!" someone else said.

Another person poked me and pointed to the photos. "They want to make copies," Thu explained. So a boy left with the photos, took them to a copier in one of the shops, and brought me back the originals. A lot had changed on the Mang Thit River in forty years.

From the edge of the ferry landing at Quoi An, I looked out at the barge traffic on the Mang Thit. It looked and sounded like 1969. The putt-putt of the two-cylinder engines was familiar. The big red and black eyes painted on the bow of the larger vessels were still visible. The loaded barges still rode low in the water looking as though a small wave could sink them, but they plow along with seemingly no worries. Islands of lotus weeds flow along with the current and the barges try to avoid the biggest clumps. All of this seemed the same to me. But the people, how they live and what they are doing, have changed. By many measures, Vietnam is still a third-world country, but its economy and its people are charging ahead into the 21st Century.

* * *

There was another aspect of South Vietnam, though, which hadn't changed: the heat. It was close to 3 p.m. when we left Quoi An and headed back in our rented sampan to meet our car and driver. I was reminded again of David Halberstam's novel, *One Very Hot Day*, about a day in the life of an American Army advisor in 1965 who was on patrol in this area of the country. It is still that way in the Mekong Delta, even in January. The heat grips you and won't let you go. I was soaked with sweat and wanted to get back to the air-conditioned car. The heat and humidity were poignant reminders of the old days, but it seemed to be hotter than I remembered. Maybe that is an indication of age. When you are young, you seem to be able to adapt to anything. As you get older, you get spoiled. Why sweat when you can be cool? When we got to the car, the driver had the A/C running.

For the next two or three hours, we drove north and west in our rental car toward the Cambodian border and the Vinh Te Canal. We crossed the southernmost large channel of the Mekong, the Bassac River, on a ferry and continued our drive north and westward, paralleling the river. As we entered the City of Long Xuyen, the cosmetics of the highway changed significantly. There was a median filled with grass and flowering plants. Thu explained that this is probably the richest province in the Mekong Delta in terms of rice and agricultural production, "so the government has more money to put into the roads." It was time to stop for the night, and we found a nice, inexpensive hotel in Long Xuyen. I had never been in this city during the war but remembered that there was an American Army field hospital here that cared for our wounded.

In the morning, after a refreshing night sleeping in air-conditioned comfort, I met Thu and Gordon in the hotel restaurant for breakfast. As I walked into the dining room, I spotted a fellow with a Western look working on his laptop computer. (It is amazing how, no matter what cultural setting you are in, similar-looking people tend to gravitate toward each other.) I walked toward him as if on automatic pilot and asked, "Are you an American?"

"No," he said, "I'm from Denmark."

"What brings you here?" I asked.

"This area of Vietnam is one of the global centers of the commercial fish farming business," he replied, and then I recalled all of the factories advertising themselves as fish processing plants that we had seen along the highway on our drive into Long Xuyen. He further explained that his company was in the food packaging industry, and that the boxes they sell are made to contain 20 pounds of frozen fish which can be shipped all over the world. "The next time you order a fish sandwich at McDonalds," he explained, "the chances are it came from Vietnam."

It is hard to grasp how all of this gets done, but somehow the Vietnamese have figured out a way to raise fish, get it processed, frozen, and on a ship to Long Beach or Oakland, California, where it can be made into fish sticks or fish burgers, and you and I can buy it for lunch for $2.69. My next question was: "What happens if the freezer unit on the container fails?"

He laughed. "First of all, you wouldn't want to be the guy who has to clean it up! But don't worry. They don't often fail. Each container of fish is worth about $70,000, so they make the units not to fail." Here I was in remote Long Xuyen meeting a Danish salesman selling packaging material for a Vietnamese fish industry whose primary customer was the American fast-food market. Forty years ago, the only fish industry I remembered were *nuoc mom* plants, factories that made a fermented fish sauce that went on Vietnamese food. When on a PBR patrol, you could smell these facilities before you could see them. Now, I was back in the same place, hearing about a fish industry that didn't exist then.

After breakfast, we loaded back into our air-conditioned SUV and headed toward our next destination, the Vinh Te Canal. The road we were on was heading toward Chau Doc, a Vietnamese city near where the Basaac River enters Cambodia, and which is also the eastern terminus of the Canal. On the outskirts of Chau Doc, we turned left on another road veering south and west toward Nui Sam Mountain. For centuries, Nui Sam Mountain has been home to a Buddhist monastery important in the cultural history of the country. Vietnamese still make pilgrimages to the site. During the war, Nui Sam Mountain was visible as we transited the Vinh Te Canal. The road continued past the monastery and toward the Seven Mountains, an area controlled by the Viet Cong during the war. As we neared the Seven Mountains, the highway turned nearly straight west and made a beeline for Tinh Bien, a commercial town on the Vinh Te Canal.

The Canal has always had historical importance. It is more than a manmade waterway used for transportation and water drainage. Prior to the time of the French, there were border disputes between Vietnam and Cambodia. Even today, there is dislike and mistrust between the two countries. In 1814, in order to firmly establish a border and encourage Vietnamese settlement, the Vietnamese government ordered the building of the Vinh Te Canal. The French made improvements in its construction, but the Canal itself is testament to ancient hatreds between old historic enemies. The legal boundary between these two countries today is, for the most part, situated just a kilometer north of the Vinh Te Canal. At one point, closer to its southern/western terminus, the Canal defines the border. It was along this same Canal that, in 1969 and 1970, South Vietnamese and American forces attempted to establish border control against the Viet Cong and North Vietnamese.

There is now a bridge at Tinh Bien that can take you to the Cambodian border. The road to Cambodia goes by a new industrial park with some newly built, large Butler-style buildings. We decided against a drive to the Cambodian border, stayed on the south side of the Canal and headed toward our old base camp at Vinh Gia. A nice two-lane road runs along the south side of the Canal. There was no road here in 1969. As we passed over a small bridge that spans a newly constructed canal, Thu told us that some of the new canal building is related to changes on the Mekong River itself. Apparently, impoundments and dams built upstream on the big river, combined with efforts to raise the banks of canals and waterways, now affect the water flows in this part of the Delta. These new canals are essentially large irrigation ditches built to release water more quickly into areas once naturally flooded. Finally, we arrived in Vinh Gia, which is just a widening in the road with houses on both sides. Situated on the dike line of the Canal, alongside the homes and shops, are the ever-present electric poles and transmission lines bringing the grid out to the very edges of the country. What I remember of the old Vinh Gia is gone. There is no fort, no military outpost. Where the Vietnamese militia base once stood is now a school, and downtown is marked by an open air bar and restaurant with men shooting pool on a table in the shade.

A few kilometers past Vinh Gia, the road and canal make a slight bend to the right heading now directly west. Here, forty years ago, we always donned flack jackets and helmets as we traveled through an area we called "blood alley," where many firefights, enemy crossings and attacks took place. Old memories come back of friends left behind who never made it home.

Yet the beauty of the place is still overpowering.

My memories of long ago are accurate. It could be a painting on your wall: rice fields, blue sky, brown water, framed by mountains in the distance. If it were located closer to the major tourist routes, it would be a "must-see" similar to what Halong Bay has become in the North near Hanoi.

The road continued west. We were told that it is well paved all the way to Ha Tien, a small town located on the Gulf of Thailand. Thu explained that some of this highway construction was defense related, that it was built as a result of Cambodia's invasion of Vietnam in 1978. In a surprise attack, Pol Pot's forces crossed into Vietnam from Cambodia and advanced as far as the Seven Mountains before they were stopped. Here, in a small village called Ba Chuc, they slaughtered everyone in the town. Three thousand men, women and children were killed. As we left the Vinh Te Canal, we stopped in this small village and paid our respects at a Memorial in remembrance of those who had died. The Memorial is reminiscent of pictures I have seen of similar places in Cambodia where collected skulls and skeletons tell the story of the Pol Pot legacy in that country.

THU, AUTHOR AND GORDON AT BLOOD ALLEY, VINH TE CANAL

The history of this area along the Vinh Te Canal reminds me of the lack of historical perspective I had forty years earlier. No one told us of the old ethnic and nationalistic rivalries along this frontier. To us, the war was portrayed as "us against them," the good guys vs. the bad guys. We had little understanding of the centuries of conflict that had occurred along this border. In 1978, five years after the end of direct American involvement in Vietnam and three years after the war ended, Vietnam was again battling the Cambodians here and was in a war with its ancient enemy, China, along its northern border. Americans tend to define history as the time between when the first American comes and when the last one leaves. The history of the centuries before our arrival and the probabilities of how that will shape the future after we leave is not something we focus on.

The road system we traveled on was better than we expected, and so we made good time after leaving the Vinh Te Canal. That night we stayed in another modest yet comfortable and inexpensive hotel in Can Tho. I had been in Can Tho many times while stationed at the U.S. Naval Base in Binh Thuy. On the highway coming into the city, we drove through Binh Thuy, and I did a double-take as we went by the old Navy base. Most of the buildings built by the Americans were still there, but Thu told us that the sign in front said, "Absolutely no admittance!" The base is now the property of the Vietnamese military.

It was a Friday night in Can Tho and the town was alive. A beautiful young girl sitting on her motorbike let us take her picture. It looked like she was waiting for her boyfriend. After dinner we walked down to the river's edge, where there is now a park and a promenade. Vietnamese families were out walking in the park, kids were kicking a soccer ball, and local vendors were selling ice cream.

As the sun set, the streetlights came on, and there were strings of lights along the sidewalks. In the middle of the park was a 30-foot statue of Ho Chi Minh. We saw similar sculpture in other towns. The statue is a reminder of who won the war, but it was obvious that it was only an ancillary part of the park. People didn't stop to gaze at it; they were too busy having fun. We finally left the promenade and headed back to our hotel.

I felt lucky. It is not often you can experience a day so filled with memories of the old combined with impressions of the new. It almost felt like overload, too much. I was tired and ready for bed.

We woke up early the next morning and walked back to the piers along the river. Thu had rented a sampan that was scheduled to leave at 6 a.m. We climbed aboard, the boat maneuvered its way out into the big Bassac River, and we headed east toward the floating market. During PBR patrols, we had often been around these markets, and they are just as interesting to observe now as they were then. Big boats come in usually carrying one or two staples like bananas or mangoes. Then small sampans, the local grocers and restaurants looking for these items pass by and an exchange price is negotiated. It is the Mekong Delta equivalent of going to a wholesale market. Once you have purchased all the produce you need for your restaurant or business, you head home. The bigger boats, the equivalent of wholesalers, then head back to wherever they came from to pick up more produce for the next day's market. It is quite amazing to see all of this happening on the open water, and the market is busiest in the early morning. On the way back to Can Tho, our sampan driver took us a few miles out of the way to see the new suspension bridge spanning the Bassac River. It is startling to see this huge structure in the middle of what otherwise is an area of low vertical relief.

It is something we could not have imagined in 1969.

Before leaving Can Tho, I asked Thu if he could find the Catholic convent where I had helped start the chicken raising operation when I was stationed at Binh Thuy. He had never been there, so we had to stop and ask people along the way if they knew where it was. Finally, someone pointed down a street.

There it was, just as I remembered. We went to the office and were met by the Sister in charge. She was very pleasant and invited Thu, Gordon and me to come in for some yogurt and tea. What had been the orphanage is still next door, but it is no longer part of the Church's activities. From what I could understand, the government took over the orphanage soon after the war ended. However, the convent was still as I remembered it. I asked our host about Sister Anicet, the well organized driving force of the convent and orphanage when I had last been in Vietnam. She said, "Just a moment," then picked up a cell phone and called a number near Pleiku.

Sister Anicet got on the phone, and we had one of those once-in-a-lifetime conversations. She was obviously surprised that I had found my way back to Vietnam. She now lives in a Catholic retirement home, and her speech is somewhat limited because of a stroke. But the memories of building and stocking that chicken coop were still strong. She kept saying, "Trung Uy, Trung Uy!" (Lieutenant, Lieutenant!) and then would break into a combination of English, French and Vietnamese. Thu finally took the phone and explained about our trip. It is not often you have the chance to revisit a place after forty years and feel like you can pick up right where you left off. Sister Anicet had made her mark. I can still see her in her spotless white habit as a Nun, directing her staff and working tirelessly to try to make a better life for those orphans so many years ago.

We thanked our host for her gracious hospitality. She had capped off a Mekong Delta Tour not available to most Americans who visit here. Our schedule called for us to be back in Saigon by nightfall, so we needed to be on our way. The rest of our trip to Vietnam would be as tourists. We had finished our visit to the rivers, canals and waterways that were home to the PBRs during that time of what is now called in Vietnam the "American War."

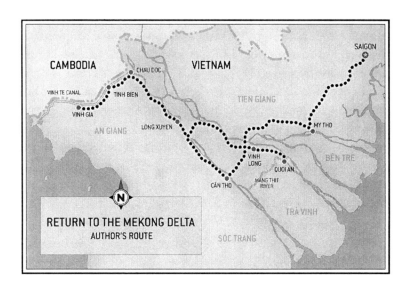

TOUR ROUTE BY CAR, 2010, RETURN TRIP TO THE MEKONG DELTA

*   *   *

When the organized tours in Vietnam go to Ho Chi Minh City (Saigon), they not only offer a day trip to the Mekong Delta, they offer other options. One is to visit the Cu Chi Tunnels, the underground labyrinth of burrowed holes where the enemy so successfully fought American troops during the war. I never experienced tunnel warfare when I was in Vietnam but had read about the "tunnel rats," the American soldiers who were sent down these holes looking for the enemy. The Vietnamese government has done a good job of preserving some of these tunnels, and it made for an interesting side trip from our hotel in Saigon. The location is unpretentious and, when you arrive, you follow a small path into what looks like a banana patch. We were met by a Park Ranger in a uniform that had a military look. He scraped some leaves from the path, bent down, pulled open a trap door and disappeared down a hole. Then he popped up out of another hole a few yards away. It provided a vivid image of what American soldiers faced when fighting the enemy in this area. I was unaware, prior to my visit, of the extent of these tunnel excavations. In this place, just outside the City of Saigon, the Viet Cong, and before them, the Viet Minh, had built 280 kilometers of underground tunnels. They were used in fighting against the French and came back into use when the Americans arrived in Vietnam. It is difficult to prevail in a foreign country when you have an enemy so determined that, if they cannot control the surface of the land, they will work to control the subsurface.

In Saigon, itself, we also visited some of the familiar sites in downtown. I declined to visit a museum which I was told was primarily an anti-American war exhibit. On the other hand, I did visit the old Presidential Palace that has been tastefully restored to the condition and times of the 1970s. A Russian tank was parked outside, reminiscent of the tank that broke through the gates in 1975 at the end of the war. Interestingly, we saw very little of the Vietnamese military on our trip—with one notable exception. I wanted to take a photo of the old American Embassy in Saigon, which is now the American Consulate. As I approached the gate with my camera, I was waved off by a Vietnamese Army soldier. "No pictures", he said. I had read in a visitor's guide that this might happen. My visit to the Consulate occurred on a Sunday, and the street and sidewalk in front of the Consulate were virtually empty. However, according to the visitor's guide, on Monday through Friday there are long lines of Vietnamese queued up on the sidewalk trying to enter the Consulate to apply for a Visa to the United States. The government doesn't like this image and so bans all photography at this location.

The next day, Gordon and I went to the airport and continued our tourist trip by plane. We boarded a Vietnamese Airline Boeing 737 and flew to Danang, now a regular stop for many tourists. We also wanted to visit an American friend who was teaching as a volunteer at the University of Danang. I had been in Danang in 1968 while serving on a U.S. Navy ship, but there is not much left to remind you of what it was like then. It is now a sprawling city. The airbase, built by the Americans, is now the city's airport, and the deep-water piers, another American-built port improvement, are crowded with commercial ships. I did find what I thought was the old "White Elephant" military headquarters building, but the rest of the town seemed totally new.

It was dusk when we pulled up to the buildings housing the University of Danang. Gordon and I had agreed, as part of our visit, to teach English for two nights at the University. It was another chance to learn what had happened in Vietnam since the war.

* * *

What grabbed my eye as we approached the school were strings of beautiful green lights that were arched over the street. It made everything look festive, and reminded me of lights that were strung over the downtown area of my hometown at Christmas time when I was a child.

Someone at the University told me, "The lights were put up by the Heineken Beer Company. The mayor wanted to beautify the area and the City didn't have the money, so the beer company agreed to do it."

I went back out to the street and looked closer. Sure enough, there at the top of the arch, on each string of lights, was the illuminated symbol of Heineken. If one wanted proof of the entrepreneurial spirit prevalent today in Vietnam, this was it. Later, after our class, we went out for dinner. At the restaurant, there were only two choices for beer: 333 Vietnamese beer (the same beer we drank in 1969, then named "33" beer) and Heineken. The lights had been a good investment for Heineken.

American veterans of the Vietnam War tend to remember the country the way it was then. But much has changed. In my return to Vietnam, I was finding a country that was thriving economically in many ways. Forty years ago, the country was positioned to become a pro-American success under an anti-communist government. It didn't work out that way. Today, it is, in many ways, an American economic success story, yet the government is communist. What it has become economically would have probably happened had their been no war.

The evidence of economic growth can be found everywhere today; new highways, bridges, urbanization and electric power. To me the country looked more prosperous than, say, the Philippines, which had no war. Vietnam has an economy comparable to that of Thailand, which also had no war.

Had we looked at Vietnam the way we did at Yugoslavia at the end of World War II, we could have recognized a Communist state with which we could do business. That is what we did with China. Yes, the Vietnamese have their problems as do the Chinese, but they have commonalities as well. They have a modern state with fantastic economic growth, but also have a feudal, one-party, top-down government.

While teaching in Vietnam, I was not hesitant to share these views. The younger generation was fascinating to me. They were eager to learn, but lacked the experience that their parents had. The old South Vietnam preserves a very pro-American attitude, but in the North, people were not quite as warm toward us. Most students have been taught that the "American War" was a conflict initiated by the United States, yet I was heartened to find that most people haven't translated that into hatred against

Americans. They realize that, in large part, it was a civil war within their own country.

The Vietnamese media is full of American news, sports, and business. For the old-timers who fought against us in the war, there is still bad feeling. But while teaching, I kept reminding myself that half the population is under the age of 35, and these young people never experienced the war.

One of most salient and positive American legacies from the war has been the manner in which the Vietnamese have embraced an open, free market system. During one of the classes, I brought up this point.

"There have been very positive advances in Vietnam, especially economically, since the War," I commented.

A young woman raised her hand. "That is all very good," she said, "but you must remember that we do not have as open a society as you do. For example, we do not allow Facebook. And we do not have the opportunity that young Americans have."

Other students were nodding as she continued, "I am in my mid-twenties and I still have to live with my parents. In America, I would have an apartment and be living on my own." I could have tried to explain that many young Americans today are returning to live with their parents as they search for jobs, but I understood her point. I saw signs of positive American influence from the war, but this was still a country that had issues with personal freedom and opportunity.

I was there to teach the students, but they were giving me a lesson as well.

* * *

In Danang, we again rented a car with a driver and drove out of the City to visit some old ruins of the Chama culture at My Son. The terrain was beautiful, and the ruins reminded me of photos I had seen of Angor Wat in Cambodia. It was raining, the foliage was lush and a clear, mountain stream wound its way through the area. This was also an area where U.S. Marines had fought during the war. There were a few bomb craters, and one of the temple buildings had been damaged in the fighting.

Just a few miles east of My Son, we visited the fishing village of Hoi An. The thousand-year old village seemed to have suffered little damage during the war and is now a major tourist stop. It is full of shops and restaurants. We went to an ATM machine, withdrew some Vietnamese currency, then sat and had lunch along one of the ancient canals that cross through the town. On our way back to Danang, we drove up the coastal highway. At China Beach where American soldiers used to swim in the surf, a Hilton Hotel was being built. Next to that, two new condominiums were under construction. The beaches of Vietnam have become a destination for the wealthy of Southeast Asia.

The following day, we drove in the rental car to Hue. The pass, north of Danang, which used to be a site of firefights, now has a highway tunnel through it to carry most of the traffic. However, we stayed on the old road just to say we had done it. As we came over the top of the pass, we were met with a magnificent view of Phu Bai and the South China Sea. A few miles beyond, we arrived in Hue, the ancient capitol city of Vietnam. We checked into our hotel which was just a block from the Perfume River. Hue is a focal point of tourism, not only for foreign visitors but for the Vietnamese. We were definitely in a tourist town. The hotel cost $100 a night, not $30 as in Long Xuyen.

The next day it was raining, so Gordon and I donned our raincoats and took umbrellas. This was going to be a day of walking in the rain. We walked across the bridge over the Perfume River, and the huge walls of the Citadel at Hue came into view. We really didn't need a map. We just kept walking toward the Citadel, which seemed to be visible from every direction. Inside those walls is where the court and government of ancient Vietnam was located. It was also inside those walls where U.S. Marines fought in hand-to-hand combat with the Viet Cong and North Vietnamese during the 1968 Tet Offensive.

Our enthusiasm about visiting this place was well rewarded. If there were a choice for the top tourist stop in Vietnam, I would recommend Hue. The place is steeped in Vietnamese history and culture. Much of it was destroyed during the War, but the restorations going on have brought new life back into the old structure of the Citadel. There is much to see. We walked through displays and exhibits for hours. For less than $10, we bought tickets to a traditional Vietnamese opera production. It continued to rain and we got wet, but it was a day to remember.

War can demolish buildings, but it can also destroy a civilized society. I was impressed to see, 40 years after this War, that the Vietnamese people had made the commitment to preserve their culture and history through an extensive reconstruction of the City of Hue.

At the end of the day, as we walked back over the Perfume River bridge toward our hotel, we spotted the steeple of a church. I stopped and looked at Gordon. "A friend of mine, Dennis, was with the Marines here in 1968. When I told him I was coming to Hue, I asked him if there was anything I should see, and he mentioned a church."

Dennis is a staunch Catholic and told me that he always felt badly because he gave the order to have artillery target a Catholic Church. There were snipers in the steeple, and the Marines decided that they had to take it down after some of their troops were shot. It had been destroyed in the fighting. As I looked at the church, I said to Gordon: "Let's stop and see if this is the place."

Late in the afternoon and soaking wet, we walked into the church. We were met by a priest who spoke relatively good English. I explained to him why we were visiting.

"Yes, this is the church that was destroyed," he told us.

I mentioned to him about my Marine friend, and he nodded. "Here, please take him this picture of the old church and this photo of the new church and steeple," he said. "Tell him not to worry. He does not need forgiveness. It was a time of war. Everything has been rebuilt. It is time to forget and move on."

Later, after returning home, when I gave Dennis the photos and told him the story, a big smile came across his face.

The following day we boarded another Vietnam Airlines flight and headed for Hanoi to continue our trip as tourists. You can feel the winter in North Vietnam in January. The weather was colder, and we needed to wear sweaters. It was also overcast most of the time. We visited Lenin Park and the area surrounding Ho Chi Minh's Mausoleum. We did not stand in line to see his remains. The small bungalow where he lived was a highlight. We visited some museums, including the large outdoor display of wrecked American airplanes and captured American tanks. The indoor displays told of American atrocities during the war. When you are the victor in war, you write your version of its history. There was one very educational display depicting the decisive victory by the Vietnamese over the French at the Battle of Dien Bien Phu. We had considered trying to travel to Dien Bien Phu, but found that it was not an easy place to get to and would take at least two days of travel. The display in the museum included a large, topographic relief map with lights that came on showing where the opposing forces were located, and how the battle progressed.

On our second day in Hanoi, we took a three-hour bus ride to Halong Bay. Any Westerner who has spent more than a week in this country has probably been here. An enterprising Vietnamese businessman saw the potential of taking people to this bay of limestone islands that jut out of an azure blue ocean. As a part of the tour, we rented staterooms on a Chinese junk that housed up to 30 people. We cruised for a day around these islands, stopped to visit limestone caves and viewed some commercial fish farms. We stayed overnight on the junk and were treated to exquisite gourmet dining. We also had the opportunity to meet other tourists who had come from countries all over the world. We enjoyed our trip to Halong Bay.

Our last night in Vietnam was spent in Hanoi, but, given the choice, I would have chosen Saigon. It was nice to visit Hanoi, but somehow it missed the warmth and dynamism of Saigon. There is something about Hanoi that seems bureaucratic and stifling but, perhaps, that is just my American bias.

*   *   *

During the tourist phase of our visit to Vietnam, I found that many of the people we met were very accessible and willing to talk openly about their country. It is still a nation caught up in its past, especially in the memories from the war. It is also a country which feels that it is on the cusp of becoming something greater and better.

As Nhi, a woman we met in Danang, told me: "There are a lot of sad stories from the war. Families lost loved ones, and many families were split between North and South." When the fighting around Danang reached her village, the decision was made that she and her mother would stay in the village, but her father and brother would leave. A few days after her father and brother left, "an American bomb or artillery shell knocked the roof off our house, and my mother decided that, for our own safety, we would also have to leave," she said. "It was good that the men in our family had gone earlier because on the boat ride back toward Danang, our sampan was stopped by some North Vietnamese or Viet Cong soldiers. They were looking for men, probably either to kill them or conscript them into their army. It was fortunate my father and brother weren't with us."

Nhi, today, is a teacher, has a grown family, and her husband is a successful businessman with strong connections in the North. Life has worked out for them, but it is clear that the wounds from the war still linger.

Hung was a tour guide whom we met in Hanoi. He spoke good English, was in his mid-thirties and is typical of the new generation of Vietnamese. He was proud of Vietnam and what it has accomplished but, along with many of his friends, is disillusioned with the scope of corruption in the country and the lack of choice in government. "You can give any policeman 100,000 Dong (about $5 U.S.), and you won't have to pay a traffic ticket," he said. "Government officials at the highest levels are rich and live well. Where does it all come from? Recently, the government spent $4 trillion Dong to build an oil refinery, but it never opened. Where did all the money go? There has been no explanation from the government."

Hung's father fought with the North Vietnamese Army during the war; his mother was a medical doctor working in a field hospital just north of the DMZ (Demilitarized Zone) treating the wounded from the American War. "Yet my father," he said, "is not happy with the way the government currently operates here. I grew up listening to war stories from my parents and their friends, but now many of them want change." Nevertheless, Hung's father cautioned his son: "It is going to take time to change things. Things cannot change until my generation is gone. The memories of the war are still too strong."

On a Vietnam Airlines flight from Hanoi back to Ho Chi Minh City for my flight home, I sat next to Lam, another young Vietnamese who spoke good English. He explained that he was "in the broadcasting business" and worked for one of the private sports channels. He had recently been in South Africa negotiating rights to broadcast the World Cup Soccer games. I commented on how impressed I was with the television I had seen. In most hotels in Vietnam, there are at least forty cable channels, including CNN, and there are four or five sports channels, most carrying soccer games. He commented that the country has come a long way economically, especially so in telecommunications. However, like Hung, he was guarded in assessing where the country is going. "You still need to have good connections in the North in order to get things done," he said, "and you have to remember that, here, the government blocks certain websites, including Facebook. We are not as open as you are in America and the West when it comes to the Internet."

In our conversation, it sounded like Lam was partial to the South. He came from the South, but now, with his job in the telecommunications industry, has moved north to Hanoi. "The South," he said, "is the economic engine for our country. Over 50% of our GNP (Gross National Product) comes from Saigon and the southern area, and I attribute a lot of that to the American influence from the time you were here. Things work differently in the North. If you pay someone in the North, usually nothing happens. At least, in the South when you pay, you get something for your money. Things get done!"

As the plane approached Ton Son Nhat airport near Ho Chi Minh City, our talk turned to the future and what it might hold for Vietnam. I brought up the fact that in Russia, after *glasnost*, the name of the City of Leningrad was changed back to its original name, St. Petersburg. I mentioned that when I checked my luggage at the Hanoi airport for the flight south, I noticed that the three-letter identification code for Ho Chi Minh City was still "SGN," just as it was when I was here forty years ago.

"Do you think," I asked, "that the city will ever again be called Saigon?"

"Maybe," Lam responded. "I don't know."

QUOI AN VILLAGE MARKETPLACE TODAY

A HOME ALONG THE MANG THIT RIVER

REBUILT OLD FRENCH CHURCH, MANG THIT RIVER

VINH TE CANAL WITH NEW ROAD NEAR VINH GIA

GIRL ON A MOTORBIKE, CAN THO

HO CHI MINH STATUE, CAN THO

YOUNG PEOPLE IN SAIGON PARK

PARK RANGER EXPLAINING CU CHI TUNNEL COMPLEX

HEINEKEN LIGHTED STREET, DANANG

WOMAN ONLINE, PHU BAI AIRPORT

WAR MUSEUM HANOI

HALONG BAY, NEAR HANOI

HOTEL UNDER CONSTRUCTION AT CHINA BEACH, DANANG

Seventeen

Flashback: The Chief

When it comes to flashbacks, I have been lucky. If it means bad dreams, I've never had them. I have a friend who was in the Marines in Vietnam, and he still has them. I have attributed some of my luck to the fact that others experienced more, or worse, than I did. Sometimes I think it is due to my age: I was older when I went to Vietnam, had read a lot about the conflict and perhaps expected to see what I saw. Could it be that I also had some good memories of the country? My exposure to combat was leavened by the fact that I also saw the good and made friends with some Vietnamese. Maybe it is DNA: I am a heavy sleeper and it takes a really bad dream to rouse me. But, for whatever reason, I feel blessed that I came back from the War without a lot of mental fallout.

That doesn't mean that I don't remember. Even on my best days, if I start thinking about Vietnam, there is always one memory that comes back: the night Chief Tozer died. The entry in my journal describing that night is quite brief, but poignant:

> *"At 0145 on 20 November 1969, I probably had the worst experience of my life. PBR 725 came into Vinh Gia all shot up from B-40's. It had been in a location I was scheduled for, until it was decided*

> *that I stay at the TOC (Tactical Operations Center)*
> *on the dike line of the canal in the little hamlet*
> *of Vinh Gia to get some experience with Mike*
> *Connolly. [Mike Connolly was commander of the*
> *heavier RAG boats, and they were getting ready to*
> *pull out of the Vinh Te Canal because the water*
> *was getting too low for them now that the monsoon*
> *was over.]*

> *"When the boat drove in, Chief Tozer was crying*
> *in agony—I had never heard anything like it*
> *but realized that they were the cries of death. We*
> *had only one Corpsman at the TOC, so I helped*
> *bandage the wounded. Chisman was in bad shape*
> *and all of the crew were seriously wounded. Tozer*
> *died. A real nightmare. Somehow I managed to do*
> *the things we had been trained to do in a first aid*
> *movie. The last we heard—all the wounded will*
> *survive. If only we could "study war no more".*
> *What a way to solve problems."*

The night started off quietly. All of the boats went out to their ambush positions along the canal. They pulled in to their assigned locations and then waited for the enemy, without incident. I was in the radio room of the command boat with Mike Connolly. We went over frequencies and procedures to be used in case artillery or air support was required. Once all of the boats were in position, we heard no more from the field. Sometime around midnight, I remember picking up a guitar that belonged to one of the RAG boat sailors and started strumming some Christmas carols. It was still a month until Christmas but, for some reason, I was in the mood to sing. The night was still quiet and that was good, but the celebration of Christmas was premature. Out of nowhere, the boat radio went off.

The first thing I heard was a machine gun going off, and then came the voice of the Chief calling me: "Five Days Charlie, we are under fire!" Then the radio went dead. I called him several times, but he didn't respond. I called a nearby boat; they had heard gunfire and what sounded like a B-40 rocket explosion. Based on that, either Mike Connolly or I called the Navy Sea Wolf frequency and asked for immediate helicopter support to come in and drop flares in the area. Within 15 or 20 minutes, the Sea Wolves were there but reported no boat visible at those grid coordinates. Then, shortly after that, I went up on deck and heard a boat engine mixed with the cries of wounded men. PBR 725 was coming into Vinh Gia.

You are never prepared for something like this. It was dark, in the middle of the night. We had only flashlights but it didn't take long to assess the damage. What amazed me most was that everyone on the boat was conscious. They were all wounded, but no one had passed out from his wounds. I knew immediately that the Chief wouldn't make it. He was crumpled in the stern of the boat with only one leg and covered with blood. He looked up at me, and in a weak voice said, "Help me, I'm dying." I told him that we would do all that we could. I asked Doc Wrather, the corpsman, to attend to him. "You will have to try and find the artery," I said. "You have had some training. Do your best." It seemed like a long time before the Chief spoke again, but it was probably only a few minutes, since he had already lost a lot of blood.

My recollection, as well as Doc Wrather's, was that his last words were:, "Now I can go be with my wife." Mike Connolly had also been on the boat comforting the Chief. Mike said that the Chief, at one point, told him: "I can't die." Later Mike would recall that the Chief was referring to his children. He needed to get home to take care of them since his wife had already died.

As Doc Wrather worked on the Chief, I turned to the others. In the film we had seen at survival school, they had told us to start with the one who appeared to be most seriously wounded. As I remember, next to the Chief, the engineman, Garold Chisman, seemed to be losing the most blood. I went to him and asked him where it hurt the most. He said, "In the back." It was then that I realized I hadn't brought a knife. The film taught us that it was usually better to cut the clothes off a wounded person than to try to take off his shirt or pants. I yelled, "Someone bring me a fucking knife!" This was not language I had learned in seminary, but they understood it in the Navy. A young Vietnamese seaman came over and gave me his knife. I started cutting away Chisman's shirt and applying pressure bandages. Then I went on to others, cutting away pants and shirts and wrapping the oozing shrapnel wounds. The boat captain, Mike Toomey, had been hit, as well as the two Vietnamese boat crewmen. The scene was living proof of how effectively a B-40 rocket could cripple a PBR boat crew.

The first two rockets had hit the port bow of the boat but didn't cause much damage. After they hit the boat, Gunners Mate Mike Morris jumped into the forward .50 caliber machine gun tub and started firing. The boat backed off the bank of the canal and turned. The third rocket came in from the back and exploded as it hit the water cooler right next to the Chief. Everyone was wounded. Morris left his guns and went to the coxwain's compartment. "It was a scene out of movie," Mike Morris explained. "I remember only steam and smoke. I couldn't see anyone except Toomey, and he said he couldn't see. The boat was bouncing against the shore and some branches were scraping against the side of the boat." Morris found that one engine had been knocked out and that the other would run only at half speed. Because Toomey couldn't drive, Mike took the controls and headed toward the base camp back at Vinh Gia. "Though the radio may have still been working, I couldn't find the mike," he recalled. "So when I got near the base camp, I hit the siren to let people know we were coming. When the boat finally nosed into the bank at base camp, the engine finally gave up. We were lucky to have made it back."

When I saw Mike Morris that night, he had a bone sticking from his leg. I assumed that his leg had been fractured. He was bleeding but not profusely. But his leg had not been fractured; it had been pierced by a bone from the Chief's leg. We patched Mike up along with the others. Heroism is not planned or practiced, it happens. The next day, we submitted Mike Morris' name to the Navy as deserving of the Silver Star for his leadership, stamina, and—indeed—his heroism in driving that boat back to the base camp on one engine with a load of wounded men on board. He recently retired as a fireman in Oregon and wears that medal to this day.

Both Vietnamese seamen were also wounded. As we finished up applying bandages and treating the wounded, one of them came up to me and spoke. It didn't look to me as though his physical wounds were as bad as some of the others. He didn't have a lot of open wounds with blood flowing. But he was eighteen years old and scared. He was only a boy. He didn't believe that his wounds were severe, but he wasn't sure. He had been in the back of the boat near the Chief, and it seemed impossible that he could have avoided so much of the shrapnel. But strange things happen in combat. One man can die while the one next to him lives, almost untouched. In halting English, the Vietnamese sailor pointed to his crotch and said: "Trung Uy, (Lieutenant) look." I had heard this about wounded men. Their biggest concern is their genitalia. What if they lose their family jewels? I had him open his belt and drop his pants. Then in my halting, pidgin English, I said: "OK, no problem, number one." He still had his balls. I hope that someday he did have kids. But, mentally, he must have been wounded somehow. No one who ever went through that night and survived would ever be the same.

It was near dawn when a Sea Wolf helicopter came in and lifted out the last of the wounded. Doc Wrather and I were covered in blood. I vividly remember taking a shower from river water and washing my clothes as the sun was coming up. The Command Boat had a pipe standing about six feet high near the stern of the vessel that the RAG boat sailors had rigged as a shower. It sucked the muddy water up out of the canal and then blew it down on you from above. I had never needed a shower so badly in my life. I was 29 at the time and Doc Wrather was in his early 20s. We had been through one of those nights that you would like to forever forget.

I didn't feel old but, I guess to those who were younger, men like Mike Connolly and me seemed like old salts. We were supposed to provide words of wisdom and solace in the midst of this carnage. Doc Wrather was in tears. He told me that he had never cried in front of anyone, but the night's events had gotten to him. He said that he had been a corpsman with the Marines in I Corps (the northern part of the country), but that he had never seen anything this bad.

"I tried, Mr. Kidder," he said. "I tried to save the Chief, but I couldn't find the artery."

"Doc, you did your best," I told him. "I am not sure anyone could have found it under these conditions." I also told him that it looked to me like the Chief had already lost so much blood that no one could have saved him, even if he had been in a field hospital.

At around 7 a.m. the boats out at their ambush locations started checking in. They had heard all of the radio traffic and knew that there had been some casualties. By 8 o'clock they began arriving at the base camp. It was my job to tell them the details and to also remind them that this was going to be just another day on the Vinh Te Canal. It would be hot as usual, we needed to grease the guns and replenish ammunition and, if possible, everyone needed to try to get a little sleep. We would be going out that night and doing the same things we did the night before. Only this time, we wouldn't have Boat # 725 and its crew, and we wouldn't have Chief Tozer. I reminded them that it is at times like this that you have to live on electrical energy or whatever energy source you can muster. We went through our usual routines finding some solace in just going through our daily chores. When something like that happens, you pull a veil over your mind, grit your teeth and keep on going. It is something you can do when you are 29. I would not want to try to do it today.

Some of the men were assigned to clean up what was left of Boat #725. It wasn't a pretty sight. Mike Morris, prior to being medivaced out, had found the fins of an exploded B-40 rocket in the back of the boat. It had to be what was left of the projectile that killed the Chief and wounded everyone else on the boat. He kept what was left of the rocket and still has it today. The Chief's remains were put in a body bag, and the last helicopter that came in took him on the start of his last journey. I had not been aware that the Chief was a Canadian. He may have told others, but he never told me. His body was heading toward the little town of Cullen's Brook on the Gaspe Peninsula of Quebec. He would be buried in a small town cemetery located about a mile from the house in which he grew up.

Life on the Vinh Te Canal went on. The war did not end with Chief Tozer's death, but a big piece had been taken out of all of us. You do not live in such close proximity, camping out for days at a time, without becoming close. These were brothers, not acquaintances. It was the luck of the draw out on that canal and everyone knew it. It could have been any of us. That night, it happened to be Chief Electrician's Mate Eldon W. Tozer who drew the short straw.

*   *   *

Memories of that night linger more with some than with others. It has never left Doc Wrather. He went on to make the Navy a career, is retired and now resides near the old Great Lakes Naval Air Station outside Chicago. Along with some other Vietnam veterans, he volunteers at the Navy Hospital at Great Lakes, now merged with the nearby VA hospital. It is called the James Lovell Federal Health Care System. They have a different name now for what we would have called combat fatigue. Today it is called PTSD, Post Traumatic Stress Disorder. However, it is same thing we knew that followed some home after they left Vietnam. Doc Wrather and his fellow volunteers are still helping people who deal with it, though, this time, the walking wounded are not coming from Vietnam. War is a nasty business and the fallout from it can have serious side effects. That is something for leaders of nations to think about before they decide to engage in it.

Eighteen

Requiem

I was once a member of a church choir that periodically sang portions of Mozart's *Requiem*. We usually did it in conjunction with remembering the members of the church who had died in the previous year. Though I enjoy it, I am no expert on Mozart or for that matter classical music. My tastes in music tend toward country-western. However, there was always something beautiful and haunting about singing this piece. We sang it in Latin, which I didn't know, so I would have to look up the words. The theme, reiterated throughout Mozart's work, was *dona eis requiem,* "grant them rest." I am sure that this would be the prayer of all who knew the three men about whom I have written who were killed in Vietnam. It is also a fitting prayer for those who never knew them.

Grant them rest.

The odyssey of remembering them started with my trip back to Vietnam. Writing about them was triggered a year later on a road trip I made to the Midwest. My journey had taken me to a lunch meeting with two of Chief Tozer's daughters in Ionia, Michigan. It seemed preordained that, before concluding my story, I would be back in the Middle West, America's heartland. I had already visited Chief Tozer's grave, then followed that with a visit with Jim Rost's family and a trip to the cemetery where Jim is buried. As I told my wife, "I can't finish this story without going to Iowa and paying my respects to Bob Olson." So a few days before Memorial Day, I boarded a flight to Chicago and rented a car. Lois Olson would be visiting her husband's grave in Britt, Iowa, that weekend and I wanted to be there.

Maybe it is the farm kid in me, but I have always felt that the force, power and strength of the United States can be seen most clearly in the mile upon mile of corn and soybean fields spread across places like Iowa. The experience is overpowering as you drive through hundreds of miles of flat, productive cropland interspersed with farm buildings and dotted with grain elevators. How could any foreign enemy prevail against this raw, productive, regenerative strength? When leaders of other nations come to the United States, they visit the big cities and Washington, D.C., but they know that there is more to America than that. They want to see the agricultural, productive strength of the country. That is why they often go to Iowa, or Nebraska or Illinois. You have to see it to believe it.

Lois advised me that probably the closest motel to Britt would be in Clear Lake, Iowa, and she was correct. I didn't know anything about Clear Lake except that it was close to the Interstate, and I could get a nice room for around $75. Though I enjoyed rock'n'roll growing up, I have never really followed rock stars and their history. Lois had told me Clear Lake was the last place where Buddy Holly played before he was killed in a plane crash in 1959, so I kept my eyes open for what might be a remembrance of that event. What I found is that it may be the biggest thing that ever happened in Clear Lake. There is a Memorial two or three miles from town where his plane went down. There is also a street named Buddy Holly Place. At the end of the street is a building called The Surf, which is where he played his last gig. It is still used as a dance hall today. I stopped in a restaurant across the street and inside were Buddy Holly photographs, including a lithographic print signed by his wife, prominently placed behind the bar. If you are a Buddy Holly fan, this is a place you should visit. It was also a nice reminder to me that even after we're gone, memories can help keep the spirit alive.

After a nice, comfortable rest in Clear Lake, I woke up early the next day and drove west toward Garner, Iowa, where Lois was staying with her companion, Don. From there we would drive another ten miles to Britt, where Bob Olson is buried. As I drove along the highway, I thought of how different this part of the country is compared to where I come from. It is not hilly and constrained. It is wide open. Though these towns have suffered from the rust-belt woes of the East, they have embraced new technologies. Windmills producing power are everywhere. There are still grain elevators, but many of them are now located near ethanol plants. I even drove past a Liquefied Natural Gas plant associated with a major natural gas pipeline. If this were in New York State, I mused, someone would probably find a way to stop all of this development.

It was a little before 8 a.m. when I turned left, drove over the tracks and came into the downtown section of Garner. Cars and pick-up trucks were already diagonally parked on the main street and breakfast was picking up at the local diners. A young man, working with an older fellow driving a Garner Public Works truck, had an armful of American flags and, in preparation for Memorial Day, was putting them on flag holders attached to the street light poles. I was overwhelmed by the Americana of it all and stopped to take a picture. I thought, "How many men like Bob Olson have come from towns like this? How many are still going into the military?" I assume that many still do. People in these towns don't wear their patriotism on their sleeves; they just do it. It is a part of who they are.

At just a few minutes past eight, I pulled up in front of Lois Olson's home. She rents it out but also keeps an apartment where she and Don stay when they come back to Iowa from Phoenix. The three of us climbed into my rental car and headed for Britt. Britt is a lot like Garner, though not as affluent. It is the home of the national Hobo Museum, and we parked right across the street from it. Lois suggested that we have breakfast at Mary Jo's Hobo House Restaurant so that I could try their "everything hash browns," a specialty of the house. Most of the people in the restaurant were our age, and many of them, like Lois and Don, go south in the winter. They were now home for Memorial Day. It is a homecoming day in Britt. During breakfast, at least half of the patrons came over to say hello to Lois and Don. Lois introduced me as a friend of Bob's from Vietnam who was writing a book. People seemed to be quite interested in that, and many of them took the time to tell me their remembrances of Bob Olson when he was growing up in Britt.

We left the restaurant and drove past the Methodist Church where Bob's funeral service had been conducted. It was not an old church. It looked the age of a church built in the boom after World War II. We also visited the house where Bob had grown up. It was small, clean, neatly kept and surrounded by cornfields. The corn was just starting to come up from spring planting. Lois Olson still owns and rents out this land. Land sales in Iowa are up, and she believes these 140 acres might be the best investment she has. At the time of Bob's death that wasn't the case, but corn land in Iowa is now a good place to have your money.

We went to the cemetery where Bob is buried. It is what you would envision a Midwest cemetery to be. The grass was well clipped, the stones square and level and there were just the right number of trees. Bob's stone is in perfect shape and his name and the dates of his life appear on a bronze plaque. Lois' name and birth date are waiting on the space next to his. Adjacent to this large stone is a much smaller one engraved with the words "The Olsons' Infant Children." Lois explained that she had miscarried several times and that, under Iowa law, any miscarried children who had been conceived for at least five months were required to be buried. Her daughter, Pam, had been adopted after her unsuccessful pregnancies.

At the end of the cemetery, just beyond the fence, was one of those water towers with the big round top that I had so often identified with towns like this. My country-western music leanings bubbled up, but I didn't say anything to Lois. However, knowing what a spark plug Bob Olson had been, I could imagine him scaling that tower in the middle of the night when he was courting her to paint *Bob loves Lois* on the side of it. In Joe Diffies' country song, the hero had painted "Billy Bob loves Charlene" on the side of a water tower in a town just like this. The act of declaring one's love on the side of a water tower seemed to be understood and accepted in the Midwestern town described in the song. It had probably been done before. According to the songwriter, the only controversy dealt with the color of the paint: "The whole town said the boy should have used red, but it looked to Charlene in John Deere green!" I don't think Bob Olson would have cared what color he used. But, when I closed my eyes, I could see him taking the risk and climbing up there and painting his and Lois' name on the side of that water tank with a big heart right in the middle.

We paused for a few minutes in front of the grave. Lois and Don held hands in silence. None of us spoke. There was nothing to say. At his Memorial service in Vinh Long on 12 August 1969, we had sung the hymn *Be Still, My Soul.* That is what we were doing now as we stood before his grave. There are only memories now, and they are mostly good ones. As I looked down at the grass beneath my feet where my old friend was buried, I said to myself, "Here lies one helluva man." But Mozart probably would have said it better. Rest in peace, Bob Olson.

**LOIS OLSON AND DON GIFFORD AT BOB
OLSON'S GRAVE, BRITT, IOWA**

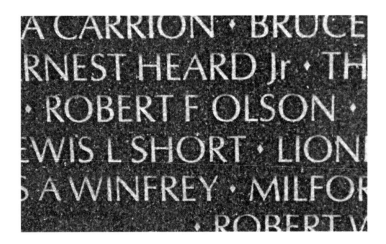

BOB OLSON'S NAME ON THE VIETNAM WALL: PANEL 20W, LINE 109

*   *   *

It was a cold, January day when I drove to Long Island to meet Jim Rost's brother and two sisters in Malverne, New York. We spent most of our time at the family home where his brother David still lives, but late in the afternoon we drove to the cemetery.

America is so different here from what I had seen in Iowa. Except for the expanse of the Great South Bay, nothing is very open. One suburban town runs into the next one, and they are all connected by expressways that originate in the mother of all towns, New York City. Communities like Malverne were built one after the other during and following World War II because more room was needed to house the veterans who were coming home from the war and starting families. Not only were cities and towns filling up, so were cemeteries. The archdiocese of the Catholic Church began to look for new cemetery locations; one of those selected is where Jim Rost is now buried.

It was about a half-hour drive to get to the cemetery. David Rost drove for a while through the suburban streets and then took an entrance ramp onto an expressway. When the signs for Republic Airport began to appear, he slowed down and took the exit ramp. I had been to the airport many years ago when I was in the state legislature, but am not sure I could have found the cemetery without David's help. When you drive to it, you parallel an old runway of the airfield and finally the cemetery appears, located on land adjacent to the airstrip. Unlike many of the old cemeteries that you see in Brooklyn or Queens, this one consists of relatively new headstones, including that of Jim Rost. Most of the graves here post-date World War II.

Jim's two sisters made it clear that this was not a place that they had often visited. "For us, cemeteries just don't seem to have the emotional pull that I am sure they had for our parents," one of them said. David gave some history on how his brother's death made a cemetery selection critical. "We really hadn't thought much about the need for a plot until Jimmy was killed," David explained. "When that happened, this cemetery was available and we selected this gravesite."

I knelt at the grave. The name "ROST" is prominent and so is the Christian cross. Jim is buried here along with his father and mother. His funeral service was held on December 1, 1969, at Our Lady of Lourdes Roman Catholic Church in Malverne. Afterward, it was to this cemetery that the Navy Honor Guard came and where the firing squad shot its three volley gun salute in memory of Navy Lieutenant Junior Grade, James F. Rost, Jr. as he was laid in the ground.

A Memorial service had been conducted for Jim Rost in Vietnam on 20 November 1969, sponsored by River Assault Division 132 and River Assault Squadron 13. It was held in Dong Tam, which was a fitting place to pay tribute to this young Naval officer. Jim had spent time there prior to his coming to the Vinh Te Canal. Dong Tam was a major staging area for the Navy's Mobile Riverine Force in the Mekong Delta. I was not able to attend the service. My hands were full from the results of the attack that had killed Chief Tozer earlier that day; I was still on patrol down on the Vinh Te Canal.

The Memorial Service, conducted by a Navy Chaplain, was simple. Old and New Testament texts were read, those present recited the Lord's Prayer, there was a short meditation and two hymns were sung. The first was "My Country, 'Tis of Thee". The second was the Navy hymn.

> *"Eternal Father! Strong to save,*
> *Whose arm doth bind the restless wave,*
> *Who bidst the mighty ocean deep*
> *Its own appointed limits keep;*
> *O hear us when we cry to thee*
> *For those in peril on the sea."*

JIM ROST'S GRAVE MARKER ON LONG ISLAND, NY

THOMAS K KAMP
JANE K PETERSON
r • JAMES F ROST Jr •
LIUS ZAPOROZEC
• OSCAR L GRIFFIN

JIM ROST'S NAME ON THE VIETNAM WALL-PANEL 16W LINE 090

When Jim Rost was killed, his sea was the brown, inland water of Vietnam. He had been in peril. It was a fitting hymn and prayer for those gathered that day at Dong Tam. The service ended with a benediction and taps. According to his sister, Jim studied Latin during his seminary prep days in high school. Had he been able to write his own funeral service, perhaps that ancient church language would have been part of the litany. Even without it, the service had power and meaning. The Navy had sent another of its sons home for burial, to *requiem aeternam,* eternal rest.

*   *   *

We left the main highway near Bonaventure, Quebec, and headed inland on a narrow town road. About a mile up the road, we passed over a small stream, Cullen's Brook. English-speaking settlers from America originally settled in this area in the early 1800s. They had been loyal to the crown during the American Revolution and came here to start a new life. Cullen's Brook is too small to be called a village; it is a cluster of homes. I didn't even see a Post Office. One of the plain, nicely painted houses we drove past, so typical of those on the Gaspe Peninsula, had been the home of Eldon Tozer.

Perhaps a half mile farther down the road, we saw a sign with an arrow that said *Cemetery.* We turned in and drove down a one-lane road with grass growing in the middle. It went through some open country and ended at the tiny cemetery. There are perhaps a hundred graves here, not more. As I walked toward the graves, I was taken by the setting. It is situated adjacent to a farmer's field, and is nudged up against a cliff overlooking the Bonaventure River. I had never seen such a peaceful setting for a cemetery. Aside from our voices, the only sounds I heard were the wind whistling in the pines and the rush of water from the river below.

Eldon's sister, Frances, didn't have to point out his grave to me. I saw it immediately. It was the only stone in the graveyard that looked familiar to me. It was white, was the same size and cut as the grave markers at Arlington Cemetery, and had obviously been sent to the Tozer family by the U.S. Navy. The marker had come from the U.S. government shortly after Eldon had been buried. It was a distinctly American marker in the midst of a Canadian cemetery. There were several Tozers buried here, the most recent being that of Eldon's brother, Winston. However, the rounded, Romanesque top of Chief Tozer's marker stood out among the graves.

Frances had explained earlier that the funeral had been a huge affair. Though Anglican, Eldon Tozer was buried from the Bonaventure Roman Catholic Church. It was much larger than the small Episcopal Church, and the local Catholic priest had offered its use to the Tozer family. Frances estimated that more than 500 people came to the funeral from all over the Gaspe. She also explained that the funeral had to be delayed for one day.

"The U.S. Navy," she told me, "had sent a color guard and firing squad from New Brunswick, Maine, to officiate at the ceremony. However, when they got to the Canadian border, customs officials stopped them from crossing because they were carrying weapons. It took a direct order from the Prime Minister of Canada to finally allow them to cross into Canada with their rifles." It was a story of frustration and bureaucracy. It was also a story of perseverance by the U.S. Navy. They had come to bury one of their own and weren't going to be turned back by a bureaucratic snafu at the border.

I thought of all of the men who had known Eldon Tozer when he was in the Navy. They would be pleased with this final chapter of his life: a grateful government, actively involved, to see that a non-citizen who had served in the United States military received a proper burial in his own country. As an American, I had a sense of pride as I stood beside his grave. I also felt that Eldon Tozer would have approved of this location. His sister had told me stories of his growing up here, of hunting in the woods and fishing in these streams, and of the family's long history of working as wardens on the Bonaventure River. Had the Chief not been buried in Cullen's Brook, I think that he would have probably retired here. The people of the Gaspe have a sense of family and of belonging to the area.

It was misty and raining the day I visited the gravesite and, in such conditions, I am usually ready to move on. However, for some strange reason, I found it hard to leave. The place somehow felt special, sacred and appropriate. It was a beautiful site high on this bluff with the river rolling past on its way to the ocean and with a backdrop of the mountains of Quebec partially hidden in the mist. There was something magnetic about it.

"After my father retired," Frances Tozer said, "he used to come here almost every night and look down at that river and remember Eldon." The life of his sailor son had been lost in a moment but the father's suffering never ended. Frances felt that her father's sorrow over Eldon's death followed him to the day he died.

ELDON TOZER'S GRAVE MARKER, CULLENS BROOK, QUEBEC

**ELDON TOZER'S NAME ON THE VIETNAM
WALL: PANEL 16W, LINE 103**

*   *   *

I doubt that there can ever be final closure for families like the Tozers, Olsons and Rosts. After all of the years, the pain is still there. We will never learn all of the lessons of war, perhaps especially those that were shaped in Vietnam. But life goes on. There is still the hope that we can learn from the past. There is also the comfort of knowing that men like Chief Tozer, Captain Olson and Lieutenant (JG) Rost responded to the call of the country and, once involved, never turned back. They knew that a military obligation, by its nature, was larger than they were. They were strong, resourceful and respected men. Those who served with them and survived still mourn their loss. The tragedy of their death is still felt deeply by their families.

As we left the Cullen's Brook Cemetery, Frances Tozer looked back and said: "I believe that if we could speak with Eldon today, he would be pleased with this site. He loved this place and the people loved him." I thought of Jim Rost and Bob Olson, and her words seemed to speak for them as well as for Eldon. They are all buried near the homes and families they loved. They are now in the care of Almighty God.

> *Requiem aeternam dona eis, Domine,*
> *et lux perpetua luceat eis.*

> Grant them eternal rest, Lord,
> and let perpetual light shine on them.

Acknowledgements

I find immense satisfaction in writing, but great frustration when it comes to publishing. As soon as your writing becomes a "book", it takes on a complexity of its own and delays become inevitable. A book, by its very nature, also becomes a joint enterprise. It takes many people to finally get it done, and the writing and publishing of <u>Backtracking in Brown Water</u> was no exception.

In terms of the writing, special thanks go to Ruth Fairbank Chiama, who edited the manuscript chapter by chapter. I also owe much to Evan Dawson who, as a published author, read it and rearranged some of the content so that it had better "flow" and improved readability. My wife, Jane, is also a good critic and helped me "stick to my knitting" and get to the point when I would tend to wander off.

There were many who kept the pressure on to finally get a finished product. Most of them were friends whom I had met in Vietnam or who were themselves Vietnam veterans. Among those who encouraged me were David Shepherd, Mel Garza, Mike Connolly, Larry Forbes, Mick Kicklighter, Max Cleland, Don Ross, Mike Paluda, Gary Holmes and Mike Morris.

Although they did not bring "pressure", so to speak, I also felt a deep sense of obligation to complete this project after meeting the families of three men I knew, the account of whose lives and deaths are related in this book. It started with my meeting

Janet and Donna, daughters of Eldon Tozer; and continued with meeting his sister, Frances Tozer Gregoire, on a trip to Canada. Later, after meeting Lois Olson at her home in Phoenix, it became clear to me that the story of what her husband had done should be put into print for others to read. Finally, meeting and corresponding with Jim Rost's siblings: David, Joan, Mary and Paul, sealed the decision to publish. To all of them, I express my appreciation for opening their hearts after all of these years to describe and reminisce about their loved ones who were lost in this War.

In terms of the graphics and layout of the book, the major credit goes to our son, Bart Goodell, for giving it the quality and professionalism it needed from a publishing standpoint. Bart has a very busy life as a designer and father of four children. The last thing he needed was for me to burden him with a book-publishing task. However, his contributions, especially in creating the dust jacket and maps, I know will be appreciated by the reader.

Finally, my deepest thanks go to Thu Trung Van. I met Thu over forty years ago when I was a Navy Patrol Officer in the Mekong Delta. The retelling of his escape from Vietnam in 1975 is a big part of this book, but, even more important, was the role he played in arranging my return trip to Vietnam four years ago. Without Thu organizing a trip back to the Mekong Delta, I would never have been able to have the perspective of what the country was then and what it has become today. His experience of leaving the country of his birth with only hours to decide, and then to "make good" in his new homeland . . . is a quintessential American success story. To have known Thu and his family over all of these years, has been one of the singular best experiences of my life.

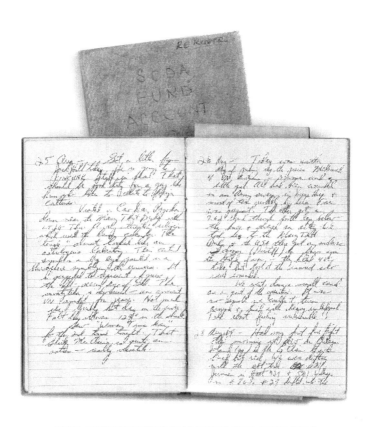

THE AUTHOR'S VIETNAM JOURNAL, KEPT IN A
REPURPOSED "SODA FUND" ACCOUNTING LEDGER

CPSIA information can be obtained at www.ICGtesting.com
Printed in the USA
BVOW05s0259070214

344180BV00001B/2/P